Rural Workers in Rural Labor Markets

RAY MARSHALL

Olympus Publishing Company ⊛ Salt Lake City, Utah

ISBN 0-913420-39-5 (Hard)

Library of Congress Catalog Card Number: 74-79847

The research from which this book emerged was supported
by a grant from the Office of Economic Opportunity and the Office
of Research and Development, Manpower Administration,
U.S. Department of Labor.

Contents

List of Tables

Acknowledgments

In the preparation of the original manuscript of this book, I am particularly grateful for the help of Calvin Beale, Vernon Briggs, Virgil Christian, Varden Fuller, Martha Gould, Niles Hansen, Dale Hathaway, Steve McDonald, Adam Pepelasis, Bert Sundquist, Tom Till, Curtis Toews, James Walker, and James Webb. Much valuable work in the preparation of this manuscript was done by Susie Turner, Jane Tonn, and Lucia Cook. I am grateful for their efficiency and cheerfulness in connection with this and other Center projects.

I have also benefited from many valuable comments by others on this manuscript. These include: Glenn Nelson, formerly with the Office of Economic Opportunity and presently with the Cost of Living Council, and Eli Ginzberg, Sar Levitan, Garth Mangum, Gerald Somers, and Robert Taggart of the National Manpower Policy Task Force, which also provided financial support for the preparation of the manuscript.

I must also acknowledge the contribution of Mike Barth and Pat Koshel, formerly of the Office of Economic Opportunity's research office, for their encouragement during the initial stages of this project, and to Ellen Sehgal and Howard Rosen of the Office of Research and Development of the Manpower Administration, U.S. Department of Labor, who took over the supervision of this project from the Office of Economic Opportunity. Others with whom I have been associated in rural projects helped me immeasurably. These include: Lamond Godwin of Rutgers University; George Esser, formerly with the Ford Foundation and now at the Southern Regional Council; Hilary Feldstein,

7

Eamon Kelly, Bryant George, and Robert Schrank of the Ford Foundation; and James Pierce of the National Sharecroppers Fund.

Although the study benefited from advice, comments, and other assistance from many sources, I alone am responsible for the factual accuracy of the material and the interpretation presented in this book.

— Ray Marshall

*Center for the Study
of Human Resources,
University of Texas*

Foreword

This book is the result of a project called "Rural Labor Markets" at the Center for the Study of Human Resources, University of Texas, wherein the author and his colleagues researched rural labor markets to determine their manpower structure, past and present, and to translate these data into an understandable doctrine readily available to the reader.

Under a grant from the U.S. Office of Economic Opportunity, later transferred to the Office of Research and Development in the Manpower Administration of the U.S. Department of Labor, Marshall and others compiled a mass of information that could indeed be the cornerstone of all subsequent endeavor in this field.

Chapter 1, "A Look at the Rural Community," gives background information and discusses problems of definition of "rural," "nonmetropolitan," or "farm." In addition, it outlines the dimensions of the rural work force. Chapter 2 concerns itself with agricultural workers and small farmers. It discusses:

(1) Major trends in American agriculture

(2) Conditions of blacks in southern agriculture

(3) Influence of outmigration from agriculture on farm-nonfarm income differentials

(4) Implications of the U.S. agricultural policy for small farmers and for blacks

(5) Future of small farmers, with emphasis on the extent to which small farmers have been displaced because of U.S. agricultural policy and the economies of size in agriculture

(6) Problems of migrant agricultural workers and several programs that have been developed to deal with migrant-worker problems

(7) Problems confronting rural workers in the Southwest because of competition from Mexican nationals

Chapter 3 examines rural, nonfarm, economic development that has been exceptionally rapid since World War II in all regions but especially in the South. The nature and location of this industrialization are analyzed to determine whether it is an urban fringe phenomenon or a growth that is taking place in distant rural counties. The chapter also discusses the extent to which various kinds of industries have provided jobs and income for blacks and underemployed whites. In an effort to measure the looseness or tightness of nonmetropolitan labor markets, the author has calculated an index for metropolitan and nonmetropolitan areas. Documentation of rural-urban and farm-nonfarm income differentials adds meat to the chapter, which concludes with discussions of the "growth center" strategy, the Rural Development Act of 1972, and the economic viability of rural areas.

Chapter 4 deals with the rural manpower programs designed to improve the operation of rural labor markets by providing more effective matching of workers and jobs. The content focuses on manpower programs that were to promote rural development, giving an overview of existing programs and discussing in detail the Rural Manpower Service, Concerted Services in Training and Education, Operation Mainstream, the "start-up training" concept, relocation assistance, and rural education, and concludes with a view of the adequacy of rural manpower outlays.

Of utmost urgency for the low-income people and small farmers is a representative organization that could promote their interests. Chapter 5 evaluates three kinds of existing entities — unions, community development corporations, and cooperatives — which, it is hoped, might articulate the needs and protect and promote the interests of small farmers and rural workers.

And finally, chapter 7 gives a brief summary of the foregoing chapters and makes recommendations for policies that might improve the economic conditions of small farmers, agricultural workers, and low-income, nonfarm residents.

The study was sponsored by the National Manpower Policy Task Force, a private, nonprofit organization primarily concerned with furthering research on manpower problems and assessing related policy issues. The Task Force sponsors three types of publications: (1) policy statements in which Task Force members are actively involved as co-authors, (2) studies commissioned by the Task Force and reviewed by a committee prior to publication, and (3) studies prepared by members of the Task Force but not necessarily reviewed by other members. Publications under (2) and (3) above do not represent the views of the Task Force or its members except those whose names appear on the study.

Members of the National Manpower Policy Task Force are:

Sar A. Levitan, *Chairman*
The George Washington University

Curtis C. Aller
San Francisco State University

Rashi Fein
Harvard University

Eli Ginzberg
Columbia University

Frederick H. Harbison
Princeton University

Myron L. Joseph
Carnegie-Mellon University

Charles C. Killingsworth
Michigan State University

Juanita M. Kreps
Duke University

Garth L. Mangum
University of Utah

Ray Marshall
University of Texas

S. M. Miller
Boston University

Charles A. Myers
Massachusetts Institute of Technology

R. Thayne Robson
University of Utah

Philip Rutledge
National League of Cities;
U.S. Conference of Mayors

Gerald G. Somers
University of Wisconsin

Lloyd Ulman
University of California, Berkeley

Phyllis Wallace
Massachusetts Institute of Technology

Robert Taggart,
    Executive Director
Washington, D.C.

The Editors

1. A Look at the Rural Community

FEW DOMESTIC problems have been more important to the nation's political, social, and economic health than those originating in rural areas. The urban migration of rural people who are not qualified by education, experience, or training for nonfarm jobs has created problems for rural and urban areas alike. To obtain better rural-urban balance, some scholars and policy makers advocate rural development to halt outmigration and to reduce rural-urban income inequalities. The most significant recent manifestation of this position was the passage of the Rural Development Act of 1972. Other observers are critical of efforts to develop lagging rural areas, arguing that these places are not economically viable. Both sides in this argument agree, however, that manpower programs must play an important role either as part of a rural development strategy or as facilitators of rural-to-urban adjustments.

Despite their importance, there is an astonishing lack of public understanding of rural problems, due in large measure to the "invisibility" of rural areas. There are few rural news media, and the only significant organized force — agribusiness — has created the misconception that "rural" is synonymous with "agriculture," or even the equally erroneous belief that farming is quantitatively the most significant rural activity. As we shall see, manufacturing provides more employment to rural people and is increasing, while farming is declining. Similarly, the fact that *agricultural* populations are declining has led to the mistaken impression that *rural* populations are declining, whereas the rural populations have been fairly constant since 1910.

13

The main objective of this book is to provide a factual and analytical basis for more effective rural development policies. Although other groups are not neglected, the primary focus is on the problems of small farmers, agricultural workers, and low-income, nonfarm workers. Because the rural poor, especially the rural black poor, are concentrated disproportionately in the South, more attention is devoted to that region than would be warranted by a study which concerned itself more with the conditions of affluent rural groups.

In addition, more attention is devoted to agriculture than is warranted by the quantitative importance of that sector in the rural economy. This is because farming, while much less important in actual amount than the rural nonfarm sector, has strongly influenced the character of rural economies, as well as the ability of those displaced from farming to shift to nonfarm jobs.

Agriculture has been a particularly important cause of rural poverty and low incomes. Moreover, even though its quantitative importance is declining, agriculture continues to be one of the nation's most important industries and is likely to remain so for as far as we can see into the future. Indeed, there are indications that the long-run rate of decline in the relative significance of agriculture in the national economy will halt and perhaps even be reversed during the 1970s and 1980s.

DEFINITIONS

There is some confusion about the meaning of "rural," which is defined differently by different government agencies. For example, the Bureau of the Census generally defines as "rural" those people living in places with populations of less than 2,500, while the U.S. Department of Labor defines it as counties where a majority of the people live in places of less than 2,500 population. The Rural Development Act of 1972 adds two more definitions:

(1) For most purposes the Act sees "rural" as meaning everything outside any city or town of more than ten thousand inhabitants (about 30 percent of the national population in 1970).

(2) For business loans and grants, the Act allows "rural" to include everything outside cities of fifty thousand population or more and their immediately adjacent urbanized areas with population densities of more than a hundred persons per square mile (about 40 percent of the U.S. population in 1970).

Special consideration is to be given to places with populations of fewer than 25,000 people.

The Census Bureau and the Labor Department define as "urban" all places that are not rural. However, "urban places" is an official census classification designating the population who are living in towns of 2,500 to ten thousand outside metropolitan areas. In 1970, some 11.3 million people lived in "urban places" in this country.

The definition problem is of much more than academic interest. Without a working definition of "rural," we are not likely to be able to devise appropriate rural policies because we will not be able to measure rural development and establish the causes of rural problems. What does it mean, for example, to say that there is more poverty in rural than in urban areas? Or that manufacturing employment is growing faster in rural than in urban areas? And what does it mean to say that rural areas have inadequate access to human resource development programs, or that urban problems have rural origins if we are unable to define rural populations or work forces?

Part of the problem involved in defining "rural" is caused by the logical difficulties in giving precise meaning to a very hazy and imprecise concept. Technology and other changes are eroding the distinction between rural and urban populations, and there is considerable diversity within rural areas.

It is important to emphasize that rural *populations* are not the same as rural *work forces*, because urban residents work in rural areas and vice versa. These rural-urban interactions have been accelerated by transportation improvements — especially improved highways — and the general availability of automobiles. We stress the distinction between populations and work forces because it is commonly erroneously assumed that declining populations mean declining work forces. As we shall see, the rural population has remained fairly constant since 1910, but the rural work force has increased steadily.

The distinction between *farm* and *rural* populations and work forces also sometimes creates confusion. Although the terms are often used interchangeably, the farm population or work force is a very small proportion of the rural work force; the rural nonfarm category is much larger and has grown by enough in every census decade since 1910 to offset the decline in the farm population and keep the rural population (census definition) constant at about fifty million.

Another term sometimes confused with rural is *nonmetropolitan*. In general, "metropolitan" or "standard metropolitan statistical area" (SMSA) refers to a county with a population of fifty thousand or more; nonmetropolitan populations include all others. The nonmetropolitan population is sometimes divided between farm and nonfarm, but this causes confusion because metropolitan areas also have farm populations. The nonmetropolitan farm population therefore does not define the total farm population. Similarly, metropolitan areas have rural as well as urban populations.

Confusion also results from special and imprecise uses of the term "rural" by government agencies and research groups. For example, a recent study used as "rural" those areas defined as rural by the Census Bureau, plus all places having populations between 2,500 and 25,000 (Abt Associates, 1970).* Others have attempted to derive functional definitions of rurality. One such measure is the hinterland concept suggested by the authors of *People of Rural America* (1968, p. 289):

> In essence, rural America is regarded as representing the hinterland of a series of metropolitan regions. The rural portions of a nation are viewed as being interdependent with the metropolitan centers, but the power to integrate, order, and control resides in the large centers. This concept of the ecological structure as applied to rural areas supersedes the long-held view of numerous local, relatively self-sufficient rural communities as the natural entities blanketing the nation.

Because of the confusion over definitions of "rural" and "urban," some authorities favor discontinuing the use of these terms, at least for research purposes. For example, Varden Fuller (1970, p. 7), a leading authority on rural manpower and agricultural labor, declares: "[For] the future, I would definitely argue against a perspective of rural versus urban as regards manpower, mobility, or occupation adjustment research."

Thus although it would be useful to have a standard and precise definition of rural, we are forced to use the definitions employed by basic statistical sources, which in general are those of the Census Bureau, but we sometimes use other definitions, especially that of the Labor Department, whenever the basic data are expressed in that form.

Although we might lack a precise definition, the concept of a "rural labor market" has some operational meaning and can be distinguished from nonrural labor markets by a number of attributes:

(1) *Sociopolitical characteristics:* Rural people depend more on informal family and friendship relationships than on formal

---

* The census definition of "urban" includes densely settled urban fringes of urbanized areas and has special rules for New England, New Jersey, and Pennsylvania, in addition to people living in towns of 2,500 or more population.

social organizations; they have governments which generally are responsive to economic elites and are not concerned with promoting human resource development, particularly for the disadvantaged. The disadvantaged and low-income groups lack effective organization and therefore have very little influence on public policy.

(2) *Economic characteristics:* Persistent labor surpluses in many markets exist, fewer employment alternatives for workers exist in rural areas, and labor market information is very poor, making it difficult to match labor demand and supply. According to Hathaway (1972, p. 8), rural people tend to "find themselves in jobs that require more than they have to offer (thus they are inefficient or mediocre performers), or they find jobs that require less than they have to offer (and they are bored, frustrated, and underpaid)."

Rural labor markets also differ from urban labor markets in having less structure; i.e., there has been less attachment of each worker to his employer; seniority, workmen's compensation, unemployment insurance, and other benefits are much less likely; and there are less likely to be collective bargaining contracts. Rural workers are much more likely than their urban counterparts to work in low-wage industry with very limited opportunities for advancement through on-the-job training.

(3) *Labor force characteristics:* Rural work forces tend to have fewer people in prime working-age categories, and rural workers tend to have less and inferior education; poor housing, health, and nutrition; larger families; higher birthrates; less skills training; higher incidences of poverty; and heavy outmigration through time. Hathaway (1972, p. 9) tells us: "In general, even if rural labor markets worked perfectly and our economy was in equilibrium, rural people would have lower incomes because the human resources they have to offer in any labor market are limited."

(4) *Rural economic activity:* The nature of this activity is different from that of urban areas. Rural employment is very closely tied to agriculture. Many jobs in small towns are likely to be dependent on agriculture, and the workers have agricultural backgrounds. Indeed there is a high probability that whatever vocational training rural populations received in their high

schools had an agricultural orientation, even though students were not destined to be farmers. Farmers are deriving increasing proportions of their income from off-farm work. Even rural manufacturing activity is likely to be distinctive — except for raw material-oriented industry, nonmetropolitan manufacturing is more likely to be nondurable goods, labor intensive, and relatively low wage as contrasted with metropolitan areas.

Rural Population and Work Force

Because of differences in definition and difficulties in counting rural populations, our information about the dimensions of the work force is far from complete. According to the census definition of "rural" in 1970, there were 53.9 million people in rural areas from a total population of 203.2 million, or about 26.6 percent of the total. The absolute rural population was about the same in 1970 as it had been in 1960; however, the total population increased by 13 percent; thus the percentage rural of the total population *decreased* from 30.1 percent in 1960.

Under the Labor Department's definition, the rural population was 45 million in 1970, or 22 percent of the total, somewhat smaller than the census definition. As noted earlier, however, the rural work force is different from the rural population because many urban people work in rural areas, and many of those who live in rural areas work in urban places. The following rough statistics for 1971 indicate the dimensions of various rural groups:

Category	Million Population
Rural population	54.0
Farm population	9.5
Rural work force	30.0
Agricultural work force	3.9
Self-employed farmers	1.84
Wage or salaried agricultural workers	1.44
Unpaid family farm workers	0.64
Seasonal farm workers	0.82
Migrant farm workers	0.18

Thus agricultural employment is a small part of the total rural work force, and hired farm labor is less than half the agricultural work force.

The relatively small size of farm populations and work forces should not obscure the importance of agriculture in the rural economy. Agriculture is important because it has dominated rural economies and shaped the characteristics of urban as well as rural populations. Similarly a large part of the rural nonfarm economy of the United States, including those who live in relatively small towns of less than ten thousand outside metropolitan areas not officially classified as rural, are dependent on agriculture.

These agriculture-related rural populations are also important because their political influence is even greater than their numbers suggest. In part, this is because of the political influence of relatively sparsely populated rural states. Although only two states, North and South Dakota, have rural population majorities, seventeen other states, including most of the South, are at least 39 percent rural, and an additional ten states are between 30 and 39 percent rural. Thus 29 states, with 58 Senate votes, have large rural blocs. Rural political strength is not as great in the House of Representatives, but it is significant even there. The National Farmers Union estimates that 85 of the 435 House districts are rural, while the Farm Bureau Foundation puts it at 65. If the "urban places" are added to the rural population, according to the Washington *Post* (p. A-16), the Library of Congress estimates that 219 House districts were predominantly rural in 1973. While these estimates do not adequately define *agricultural* political power, that power clearly is significant.

For all of these reasons, those interested in rural labor markets should not exaggerate the importance of agriculture, but they should not neglect this important sector either.

References

Abt Associates, Inc. *The Causes of Rural-to-Urban Migration among the Poor.* Cambridge, Massachusetts: Abt Associates, Inc. 1970.

Fuller, Varden. *Rural Worker Adjustment to Urban Life.* Ann Arbor, Michigan: Institute of Labor and Industrial Relations, University of Michigan-Wayne State University, and National Manpower Policy Task Force. 1970.

Hathaway, Dale. "Some Special Characteristics of Rural Areas." In *Labor Market Information in Rural Areas.* Edited by Collette

Moser. East Lansing: Michigan State University, Center for Rural Manpower and Public Affairs. 1972.

Hathaway, Dale E., Jr.; Beegle, J. Allan; and Bryant, W. Keith. *People of Rural America*. U.S. Department of Commerce, Bureau of the Census. 1968.

Washington *Post*, March 19, 1973.

2. Agricultural Employment: Changes in Rural America

THE WHOLESALE displacement of farm populations has been one of the most dramatic domestic developments since World War II and has created some serious human resource development problems. The proportion of farm residents to the total population declined from about 25 percent in 1940 to about 5 percent in 1970, and the farm population declined from 30.5 million to 10.3 million during this period. The displacement of the rural black population was particularly portentous.

In 1950, blacks and other minorities constituted 16 percent of the farm population, as compared with only 10 percent in 1969 (*Manpower Report*, 1971, pp. 113–43). However, these figures do not mean that the rural population has declined because, as noted in chapter 1, the rural nonfarm population increased slightly between 1960 and 1970. Thus despite consistent migration from agriculture, the *rural* population remained at approximately the same number between 1960 and 1970. Moreover, higher rural birthrates and the probable continued mechanization of agricultural crops — which have been major factors in the displacement of agricultural labor — are likely to continue during the 1970s, although the displacement from agriculture is likely to be at a reduced rate.

Labor requirements in agriculture have declined primarily because of rising productivity. Between 1947 and 1969, farm output per man-hour increased by 260 percent, while nonfarm output per man-hour increased by only 82 percent. As a consequence, total farm output increased by 50 percent, even though the number of farms declined by 50 percent. Although the planting and harvesting of some crops (such

21

as cotton) have been fairly thoroughly mechanized, many technological breakthroughs in these procedures for tobacco, fruits, and vegetables have not been thoroughly exploited and probably will cause considerable displacement of labor during the 1970s. The known changes in harvesting flue-cured tobacco alone will have a serious effect on workers in the tobacco-producing areas of the South, because tobacco has been a labor-intensive crop that was singularly helped by U.S. agricultural policy (Economic Research Service, 1969).

Another significant development for labor markets has been the decline in the numbers and the growing average size of farms. Mechanization and consolidation of farms reduced the number from about six million in 1947 to nearly three million in 1970. The average farm size increased from 196 to 387 acres during this period, and larger farms increased their proportion of total cash sales. In 1960, only 13 percent of all farms had sales of $20,000 and over, and they accounted for a little more than half of farm sales; by 1969, farms in this category had increased to 19 percent of all farms, but they now accounted for almost three-fourths of farm sales.

These developments in agriculture have increased the nation's agricultural output, but they have also created many problems for human resource development because many of the displaced workers have inadequate education and training for nonagricultural jobs. Moreover, the best educated and most adaptable portion of the rural population tends to move to urban areas, leaving behind many people who are unable to compete either with larger agribusinesses or for rural jobs. In 1970, some 45 percent of the nonmetropolitan population aged 25 and older had had eight years or less of education, but only 25 percent of the people in metropolitan areas aged 25 and older had had eight years or less of education. Moreover, about three-fourths of all black farm residents had had eight years or less of school. Rural populations also have relatively fewer people of working age. In 1969, 25 percent of the nonmetropolitan and 33 percent of the metropolitan population fell in the prime working-age group (ages twenty to 44).

These developments have caused some significant changes in rural employment patterns. For one thing, large numbers of small farmers and tenants have been transformed from farmers to agricultural workers. Between 1950 and 1969, 2.3 million full-time equivalent jobs were eliminated from southern agriculture alone. For the nation as a whole, farm laborers constituted 20 percent of male workers outside metropolitan areas in 1960, but only 14 percent in 1969.

These changes also reduced the distinctions between farm and non-farm workers. In 1960, 33 percent of farm residents worked primarily off the farm; this proportion had increased to 43 percent in 1969. As we shall see later in this chapter, farm operators received 52 percent of their income from nonfarm sources in 1970. Improved roads and better communications made it possible for farm residents to commute to nonfarm jobs and for urban residents to commute to farm jobs.

The main problem for human resource development in rural areas is widespread underemployment and poverty. In 1969 half of the poor but only a third of the population lived outside metropolitan areas. The poor constituted a fifth of rural, a tenth of city, and a fourteenth of metropolitan populations. Moreover, the rural poor were relatively worse off in terms of income levels — average poor family incomes in 1969 were $2,125 in metropolitan areas, $1,973 outside metropolitan areas, and $1,169 for farm families. Living costs might have been lower in rural areas, but this is offset somewhat by larger sizes of farm families.

Thus the pattern that emerged in American agriculture by the early 1970s was considerable mechanization, growing farm sizes, and rising incomes for some rural residents, but low incomes and underemployment for many others. Moreover, the people remaining in rural areas seemed to have many disadvantages for human resource development purposes: They were old or very young, had larger families, had less and inferior education, or were minorities. In addition, they tended to be economically and politically disorganized and powerless, causing public policies that vitally affect them to ignore their interests.

FARM TENURE AND OFF-FARM INCOME

The 1964 and 1969 Census of Agriculture provides detailed characteristics and trends of farm operators. As Table 2-1 shows, the number of black-operated farms in the South declined from 183,638 in 1964 to 84,469 in 1969, or a decline of 53.8 percent, as compared with a total decline of only 14.8 percent. However, only 24,144 of the black-operated farms were in class 1-5 (i.e., with sales of $2,500 or more). The greatest relative decline in black-operated farms was in the tenant classification. Black full owners of class 1-5 farms probably increased, though statistics are not available for 1964. Among all races, there was a sizable increase (35 percent) of full owners, a slight decline in part owners (−7.2 percent), and a large decline in tenants (−43.2 percent).

The changes in total acres operated by all farm operators and by blacks between 1964 and 1969 are shown in Table 2-2. It is clear from

TABLE 2-1

Changes in Farm Numbers of Thirteen Southern States,
by Tenure, Class, and Race*
(1964–69)

| Category | Number | | Percentage of Change |
	1964	1969	
All farms:			
Full owner	764,985	746,729	– 2.4%
Part owner	293,864	237,992	–19.0
Tenant	247,385	132,745	–46.4
TOTAL	1,306,234	1,117,466	–14.8
Class 1-5 farms: **			
Full owner	218,414	296,658	35.8
Part owner	195,532	181,450	– 7.2
Tenant	142,961	81,272	–43.2
TOTAL	556,907	539,380	– 0.1
All black-operated farms:			
Full owner	69,876	52,062	–25.5
Part owner	30,187	15,236	–49.5
Tenant	81,735	17,166	–78.4
TOTAL	182,638	84,464	–53.8
Class 1-5 black-operated farms: **			
Full owner	NA	9,793	
Part owner	NA	7,474	
Tenant	NA	6,877	
TOTAL		24,144	

NA=not available.

* The states are: Alabama, Arkansas, Florida, Georgia, Kentucky, Louisiana, Mississippi, North Carolina, Oklahoma, South Carolina, Tennessee, Texas, and Virginia.

** Class 1-5 includes all farms with $2,500 or more in sales.

SOURCE: Bureau of the Census, U.S. Department of Commerce; *U.S. Census of Agriculture, 1969* and *U.S. Summary of County Reports,* Tables 1 through 14.

TABLE 2-2

Changes in Total Farmed Acreage of Thirteen Southern
States, by Tenure, Class, and Race*
(1964–69)

Category	Acres (thousands)		Percentage of Change
	1964	1969	
All farms:			
Full owner	123,937	137,432	10.8%
Part owner	143,184	143,201	
Tenant	44,105	44,358	0.6
TOTAL	311,226	324,991	− 3.6
Class 1-5 farms: **			
Full owner	NA	98,262	
Part owner	NA	135,821	
Tenant	NA	40,402	
TOTAL	261,685	274,485	4.9
All black-operated farms:			
Full owner	4,426	3,807	−14.0
Part owner	2,694	1,717	−36.2
Tenant	3,000	885	−70.5
TOTAL	10,120	6,409	−42.6
Class 1-5 black-operated farms: **			
Full owner	NA	1,405	
Part owner	NA	1,416	
Tenant	NA	542	
TOTAL		3,363	

NA = not available.

* The states are: Alabama, Arkansas, Florida, Georgia, Kentucky, Louisiana, Mississippi, North Carolina, Oklahoma, South Carolina, Tennessee, Texas, and Virginia.

** Class 1-5 includes all farms with $2,500 or more in sales.

SOURCE: Bureau of the Census, U.S. Department of Commerce, *U.S. Census of Agriculture, 1969* and *U.S. Summary of County Reports,* Tables 1 through 14.

Tables 2-1 and 2-2 that fewer white farm owners are farming much more land, whereas for blacks, both the number of farms and the acreage have declined. In 1969, the average black farm in class 1-5 was 139 acres, as compared with 400 acres for all farms.

Displaced farmers are not moving entirely to nonfarm jobs but are supplementing their farm income with off-farm work; 58.1 percent of all farm operators reported off-farm work in 1969, up from 48 percent in 1964. The proportion of black farm operators who reported off-farm work rose from 41 to 53.7 percent during this period.

These figures confirm a national trend for farm operators to engage in more off-farm work. Indeed, in 1970, U.S. farm operators got 52 percent of their income off the farm (Economic Research Service, July 1971). The proportion of off-farm incomes varied inversely with income from farming: Farms with net farm sales of $40,000 and over got only 18.4 percent of their income from nonfarm sources, whereas farms with sales between $5,000 and $9,999 had 58.8 percent off-farm income. Farms with net sales of $2,500 to $4,999 got 72.7 percent of their income from nonfarm sources, and those with sales of less than $2,500 had 88.3 percent of their income from nonfarm sources.

The proportion of nonfarm income for all classes of farms has increased, as shown in Table 2-3. These statistics indicate that farms with less than $10,000 in net sales have switched largely to nonfarm sources of income, a factor which further reduces the distinction ordinarily

TABLE 2-3

Percentage of Nonfarm Income for All Classes of Farms
(Selected years)

| | Percentage of Total Income | | |
Value of Net Sales	1960	1965	1970
$40,000 and over	10.3%	14.9%	18.4%
$20,000 to $39,999	16.2	20.2	26.0
$10,000 to $19,999	19.0	27.2	35.7
$5,000 to $9,999	31.0	47.8	58.8
$2,500 to $4,999	48.5	63.8	72.7
Less than $2,500	76.3	82.7	88.3
All farms	41.9	47.2	52.0

SOURCE: Economic Research Service, U.S. Department of Agriculture, *Farm Income Situation* (July 1971), Table 5-D.

drawn between farm and nonfarm employment. In 1970, some 1.11 million farms had sales of $10,000 and over, and 1.689 million farms had sales below that amount.

Because of the large proportion of off-farm income, those farms with relatively small farm sales had higher average incomes than those in the middle ranges, which had greater reliance on farm income.

DISPLACEMENT OF BLACKS FROM SOUTHERN AGRICULTURE

Data from the 1967 Survey of Economic Opportunity, funded by the Office of Economic Opportunity, provide some insights into the rural-urban adjustment of blacks, as well as the effects of migration on the urban areas to which blacks migrate and the rural places from which they migrate (Beale, May 1971, pp. 302–07). These data confirm the general impression that the best educated blacks tend to migrate. While only 16 percent of rural blacks seventeen years of age and over were high school graduates in 1966, 26 percent of rural-urban migrants were high school graduates. The median education level for rural blacks was eight years, as compared with 8.8 years for migrants and 10.9 years for urban-born blacks.

However, these figures are misleading in the sense that migrants have a higher age distribution than urban-born blacks. If we compare blacks younger than thirty, migrants have about the same education levels as the urban-born. Migration thus tends to lower the median education levels of blacks remaining in rural areas. In the seventeen to 29 age group in 1967, half of rural high school graduates migrated to urban areas; only a sixth of those with eight years or less of education migrated.

The survey data also provide some information on the relative welfare and ease of adjustment of blacks who migrate, as compared with those who are urban-born or who remain in rural areas. The median income of black migrants in 1966 was $5,116, as compared with $5,105 for urban-born natives. However, 74 percent of migrants and 69 percent of urban-born heads of families were males; when the numbers are adjusted for sex, the urban-born earned $300 more in 1966 than the migrants. The difference in the incidence of poverty was also insignificant: 26.6 percent for migrants, 26.9 percent for the urban-born, but 57.7 percent for rural nonmigrants.

The survey data also indicate that blacks do not move out of the poverty category as fast after they migrate as whites in the same age groups who migrated at the same time. For example, of people between thirty and 49 years of age in 1966 who migrated from rural areas before 1940, the incidence of poverty was only 1 percent for whites but 18.6 percent for blacks. The incidence of poverty for those who moved during the 1960s was 8.5 percent for whites and 21.8 percent for blacks. Thus whites apparently move out of poverty fairly rapidly, but blacks who migrated twenty years ago have about the same incidence of poverty as recent arrivals.

We do not know the extent to which displacement of the agricultural labor force in the South has run its course, but the small numbers remaining on the farms will cause future displacements to be small in comparison to those of the past. The technological revolution in cotton production, where half of all black operators have been concentrated, is nearly complete, as indicated by aggregate man-hours in production in 1966, only 14 percent as great as in 1940 (*Changes: Summary*, 1967, p. 13).* But future labor use in tobacco, where a fourth of black operators are, is uncertain because of potential changes in production methods and uncertain demand.

The racial breakdown of the number of workers and full-time man-years of work required in southern agriculture from 1950 to 1969 indicates the extent of displacement and hidden unemployment. The difference between the number of workers and full-time jobs provides a rough measure of hidden unemployment in southern agriculture. In 1950, some 2.74 million white workers filled 1.96 million farm jobs, or about seven jobs for ten workers. By 1969, however, 1.19 million white family farm workers filled 59 million jobs, or less than five jobs for ten workers. There were about 767,000 nonwhite family farm workers in 1950 and 540,000 nonwhite full-time jobs, about the same ratio of workers to jobs as for whites. However, by 1969, there were about 158,000 nonwhite workers and only 73,000 full-time jobs, a ratio of about 4.6 jobs for every ten workers. Hidden unemployment had therefore increased for both racial groups, but more for nonwhites.

Breaking down the farm family worker series by race also confirms that black farmers have been displaced at a much greater rate than white farmers (operators and unpaid family workers). In 1950 there were three blacks for every ten whites, but by 1969 there was less than one black for every seven whites. Thus there were approximately 30 percent as many white farmers in 1969 as in 1950, but only 13 percent as many blacks.

---

* Man-hours are reduced to a homogeneous equivalent in the series and reflect the labor needed to produce the actual output.

Hired farm labor also dwindled sharply over these two decades, the numbers of workers having dropped from 1,043,000 in 1950 to 513,000 in 1969 (*Changes*, 1969). The decline of 530,000 amounts to roughly 453,000 full-time jobs; USDA data show that the average workweek for hired labor in the South is 34.17 hours, or 85.42 percent of a forty-hour week (*Farm Labor*, 1967). The amount of full-time employment in 1969 — 438,000 jobs — in the region apparently was split almost equally between the races (Agricultural Economics Reports).* Reduction in the two full-time equivalent series (1,838,000 for family workers and 453,000 for hired farm workers) gives a total loss of 2,291,000 agricultural jobs, divided in the approximate proportion of seven white to three black.

The loss of 2.29 million agricultural jobs put considerable pressure on rural people of both races and also on the regional economy. The magnitude of the pressure is shown by the fact that the agricultural job loss amounted to 14 percent of total nonagricultural employment in 1967.

A major reason many blacks displaced from agriculture have not been absorbed in the nonfarm economy is their lack of adequate training, education, and experience for nonagricultural jobs. Our analysis suggests that more than 80 percent of the black males who left southern agriculture during the 1960s had less than an effective seventh grade education (white equivalent), and over half had less than four years.

The white picture was better but still far from adequate. In 1960 in the South, 71.4 percent of white farm males had less than high school, 46.4 percent had less than eight years, and 19 percent had less than five years. Detailed studies of the Mississippi Delta and South Carolina for 1966 reveal that more than three-fourths of the black poor and 63 percent of the white poor had seven years of education or less in the Delta. The figures for the nonpoor were 55 percent of blacks and 32 percent of whites. For South Carolina, 82 percent of the black poor and 60 percent of the white poor had seven years of schooling or less; the proportions for the nonpoor were 53 percent for blacks and 27 percent for whites (McCoy, 1970).

MIGRATION AND INCOME DIFFERENTIALS

If agricultural labor surpluses depress agricultural incomes below the earnings of comparable nonfarm resources, traditional economic analysis would predict a number of equilibrating changes. For one

---

* These percentages are for the census South.

thing, increasing agricultural productivity might lead to declining prices, increasing agricultural sales and therefore offsetting the decline in the amount of labor demanded in agriculture. However, the price elasticity of demand for agricultural products is such that declining prices will not produce enough additional sales to offset the effects of increasing productivity, and the income elasticity of demand for agricultural products is such that rising incomes probably will not lead to increased sales sufficient to absorb the increased aggregate output. Although there will continue to be some increased consumption of farm products, not much adjustment in agricultural labor surpluses can be expected from the domestic demand side under pricing arrangements that prevailed before 1973. However, rising international demand could increase the demand for agricultural products and labor. If the demand for agricultural products does not increase, labor surpluses can be reduced only by the movement of workers from farm to nonfarm jobs. If nonfarm jobs exist in rural areas, the adjustment might be made by supplementing farming with nonfarm income. If farm-nonfarm or rural-urban income inequalities persist, it must be mainly because of one or a combination of the following:

(1) Agricultural labor is less productive than nonfarm labor; therefore the lower earnings are due to lower productivity, while wage rigidities in agriculture prevent wages from falling to the level of their marginal productivity. In this case, there is no misallocation of labor between farm and nonfarm sectors, and the remedy for low agricultural (or rural) incomes is to increase the productivity of labor and not merely to increase migration.

(2) There are impediments to the movement of labor out of agricultural or rural occupations which should be removed to facilitate mobility and reduce income inequalities.

(3) The movement from farm to nonfarm or rural to urban employment is not responsive to income differentials; in which case, workers in agriculture or rural areas have noneconomic or psychic incomes which tend to equalize wages.

Many studies indicate that although farm outmigration is motivated mainly by economic considerations, noneconomic factors are also at work, and many of those who migrate do not in fact gain from migration. Using Social Security data, Hathaway and Perkins (1968, p. 203) found that 40 percent of those who migrated from agricultural to nonagricultural occupations lost income the first year, and many of those who lost income returned to farm employment. Moreover, the first-year gains of migrants were inversely related to age: migrants over 45 years of age were more likely to lose the first year, and those under 45 were more likely to gain (Perkins and Hathaway, 1966, p. 203).

However, it should be emphasized that these studies refer to *occupational* and not *geographic* mobility because many of those who change from farm to nonfarm occupations do not move their residences. For example, in a study of farm-to-nonfarm mobility in the period 1957 to 1960, it was found that nearly half of those who changed from farm to nonfarm occupations sustained losses in earnings and that two-thirds of those who changed from farm to nonfarm employment did not migrate. Nonmigrants were most likely to be those who were from low-income areas. Workers from those areas therefore relied most heavily on local labor markets (Hathaway and Perkins, May 1968, pp. 342–53).

As noted earlier, data from the Survey of Economic Opportunity provide some information on the ability of black rural-to-urban migrants to function in urban labor markets. This and other research confirm a surprising but consistent finding that blacks who migrate from the rural South to the urban North apparently have equal or greater employment and income stability than blacks with the same attributes born in those urban areas or blacks who move there from other northern urban areas (Beale, 1971; Masters, 1970).

There is some evidence, moreover, that those migrants who remain in urban areas for some time experience gains after a period of adjustment. Wertheimer (1970), for example, estimates (by means of regressions in which gains to migration are estimated as differences in expected income between migrants and nonmigrants, where age, sex, race, and migration status are independent variables) that except for cities of 750,000, there were no gains from migration the first five years, but during the next thirty years, earnings differences ranged from $550 per year for cities smaller than fifty thousand to $1,675 per year for cities of over 750,000. The present value of the expected earnings differential at age twenty ranges from $3,650 for small to $12,500 for large cities.

Wertheimer's results show greater gains to migration than many other studies. His results are due to: (1) his sample, which was heavily weighted by the poor and nonwhites, whereas the Hathaway and Perkins' studies used Social Security data, which excluded those too poor to qualify for Social Security; and (2) his technique, which controlled for education, age, race, and sex. His results for the first five years (no gains to migration) are similar to the short-run results of other studies (McDonald, 1971, p. 20).

Many studies have found farm-nonfarm migration to be strongly influenced by nonfarm unemployment. Indeed nonfarm unemployment appears to be a more important determinant of off-farm migration than income differentials. High nonfarm unemployment influences migration by discouraging outmigration, by inducing a return to farming of many previous outmigrants who lose their nonfarm jobs, and by reducing the prospective returns to outmigration (Bishop, 1961; Sjaastad, 1961, p. 15). Blacks seem to be particularly handicapped in finding nonfarm employment during recessions (Hathaway and Perkins, 1968).

Although there is some disagreement over its significance, most students of labor markets seem to consider inadequate information to be an important deterent to mobility. Paul Johnson (1968, pp. 238–47), for example, concludes that this is "probably the most important constraint" on the movement of the rural poor. It is well known that blacks and southern whites depend heavily on friends and relatives for information; a study by Smith (1966, p. 817) confirms this. He found that most migrants came to Indianapolis with information of a very low quality.

McDonald reviews a number of studies which show that massive outmigration has not tended to reduce either the farm-nonfarm income gaps or income inequality within agriculture (Hathaway, 1967; Bishop, 1967). However, as will be shown later, these studies were based mainly on pre-1960 data, and there is evidence that rural-urban and farm-nonfarm income gaps narrowed during the 1960s.

As noted earlier, the persistence of the farm-nonfarm income differentials can be explained either because (1) farm workers have substantially less earning capacity than urban workers, (2) farm workers lack response to the economic incentives, or (3) impediments to farm outmigration exist. There is substantial support for the first proposition (Hathaway and Perkins, May 1968; Fuller, 1961, pp. 28–35; Blau and Duncan, 1967, pp. 277–94). However, other authorities disagree with this finding and conclude that the earning capacity of farm labor, when adjusted for such factors as education, age, and sex, is not very much less than that of nonfarm workers (Bishop, 1967; Johnson, June 1953, pp. 296–313; Wertheimer, 1970).

The failure of many migrants to gain relative to similar groups who do not move casts some doubt on the efficacy of outmigration alone as a way to solve the problems of inadequate rural incomes. The exaggerated income gains for rural-urban migration result in part from a failure to control for those income-earning characteristics (age, education, sex, and so forth) more likely to be found in migrants than rural non-migrants. Moreover, most studies of the economic gains from migration seem to greatly underestimate the cost-of-living differentials between rural and urban areas (which could be substantial, although we have no appropriate measures). Noneconomic costs of movement, which evidently are greater for older migrants than for the young, must also be considered.

Other impediments to rural-urban migration are imposed by various labor market and social constraints. With respect to labor markets, it is very difficult for workers with limited skills and education to break into other than marginal nonfarm jobs, particularly when skilled workers are unemployed and workers with higher levels of education are available. The returns to migration apparently outweigh the costs only for younger, better educated workers who remain in nonfarm work long enough to acquire some job experience. Although they apparently gain considerably as compared with their situation in the rural South, blacks who migrate to urban areas also face the problem of racial discrimination by employers and other labor market institutions. Inadequate job information undoubtedly is an obstacle to mobility, although its importance in the total complex of impediments is difficult to measure. The lack of nonfarm job information in rural areas has been perpetuated by an agrarian tradition which limits their access to the range of occupational information available to urban residents and because of the difficulties involved in extending manpower services to thinly populated rural areas.

U.S. AGRICULTURAL POLICIES

There are few if any areas of U.S. domestic policy where inadequate planning and neglect of human resource development have had greater consequences than agricultural and rural development policies. Our failure to safeguard the economic and political security of blacks, beginning with emancipation, permitted conditions in the South where blacks had great difficulty educating themselves and developing their productive skills. Consequently, they were generally forced either to lead precarious existences in rural areas or to migrate to cities where urban miseries were substituted for rural ones. Although the conditions of blacks were worse, many poor whites and chicanos were only slightly better off. They, along with blacks, also have had very little power to influence agricultural, immigration, or other policies with important implications for their welfare. Agricultural policies generally have displaced the poor of any race or ethnic background and have done virtually nothing to prepare displaced agrarians for alternate employment.

The first significant effort to do something for the rural poor was during the New Deal period of the 1930s, when a number of agencies, especially the Resettlement Administration and the Farm Security Administration, attempted to help poor people through land reform and resettlement, rural rehabilitation loans, cooperatives, improved tenure leases (to prevent landlords from cheating tenants and small farmers through very "loose" contractual arrangements), emergency grants and loans, medical care and sanitation, migrant labor camps, and other measures designed to help persons displaced from agriculture.

Although these New Deal measures did something to help the rural poor, they made small impact on their needs and were more than counteracted by the adverse effects of other policies which tended to displace small farmers and sharecroppers. Particularly disastrous for poor farmers was the Agricultural Adjustment Act, which sought to stabilize farm income by limiting the acreage of cash crops, removing agricultural surpluses from the market, paying agricultural subsidies, and promoting resource conservation. Unfortunately, however, these measures primarily benefited larger farmers who had sufficient land and capital to take advantage of their provisions . . . these measures amounted to land and capital subsidies which displaced labor. Simultaneously, the land grant college system, responding to the interests of larger commercial farmers, developed plant and livestock strains and machines which were not adaptive to the uses of small farmers and which therefore reduced agricultural labor requirements (Myrdal, 1944, p. 256; Maddox, 1968; Benedict, 1953; Baldwin, 1968; Conrad, 1965; and Grubbs, 1971).

Although justified on the grounds of "parity," agricultural programs have continued to most help those who need help the least. Agribusiness interests have been able to perpetuate their control over the system through a constellation of political and economic powers extending from Congress to the local sheriff's office. The system has been particularly detrimental to black farmers.

The large-farmer bias of U.S. agricultural policy is clear, although the degree of that bias is difficult to measure. By subsidizing land and capital, agricultural programs gave advantages to farmers with much capital and land relative to those who primarily had labor. This is not to deny that agricultural policies have had some beneficial effects on small farmers. On the whole, these programs apparently have reduced the inequality of wealth and income, because the distribution of income is more unequal than the distribution of the agricultural subsidy system. Similarly, to the extent that subsidies were capitalized, the system sustained land values and made it possible for small farmers to minimize their losses from shifting out of subsidized agriculture.

With respect to the distribution of agricultural subsidies (price supports and direct set-aside payments), Table 2-4 makes it clear that the distribution of benefits not only was extremely unequal in 1964 but also generally became more regressive between 1964 and 1971. The top 20 percent of benefit recipients got more than half of the benefits for all crops except corn in 1971 and tobacco in 1968. The best overall measure of inequality is in the Gini ratio, where zero is perfect equality and 1 is perfect inequality. Not only were the benefits from most crop subsidies (except tobacco) extremely unequal, but the degree of inequality for the wheat, cotton, and peanuts programs increased between 1964 and 1971. Figures for the tobacco program were not available for 1971, but the

TABLE 2-4

Distribution of Benefits from Price Supports and Direct
Payments Subsidies, by Size of Recipient
(1964 and 1971)

Crop	Largest 20 Percent		Smallest 20 Percent		Gini Ratios*	
	1964	1971	1964	1971	1964	1971
Rice	65	59	1.0	2.0	0.622	0.575
Wheat	63	71	3.0	4.2	0.569	0.647
Cotton	69	72	1.8	2.5	0.653	0.683
Peanuts	57	72	3.8	2.3	0.454	0.695
Tobacco	53**	47†	3.9	7.6	0.470	0.420
Corn		45		2.1		0.588
Grain sorghum		52		8.7		0.493

* In this ratio, zero is perfect equality and 1 is perfect inequality.

** For the year 1965.

† For the year 1968.

Source: Figures for 1971 are calculated from U.S. Department of Agriculture data; those for 1964 are from James Bonnen, "The Distribution of Benefits from Selected U.S. Farm Programs," in President's National Advisory Commission on Rural Poverty, *Rural Poverty in the United States* (Washington, D.C.: U.S. Government Printing Office, 1968).

relative equality in benefits from this program is due to some extent to the fact that the tobacco subsidy system before 1971 was unique in perpetuating small-scale holdings. This was due to the labor-intensive nature of tobacco harvesting and production and the acreage allotment system, which required that land and allotments be sold together, unlike the cotton system, where allotments could be purchased separate from the land and concentrated on large acreages. However, technological changes in tobacco, especially the development of the mechanical tobacco harvester in the late 1960s and early 1970s, and the change in the allotment system in 1971, undoubtedly give strong impetus to the growth of larger tobacco farms. This could be a particularly important problem for black farmers, 25 percent of whom traditionally have been in tobacco.

Despite technical measurement problems that make it difficult for us to determine the extent to which policy has displaced small farmers, there can be little doubt that the subsidy system has had a *net* effect of displacing smaller farmers.

The Agricultural Stabilization and Conservation Service (which administers agricultural price supports, establishes acreage and crop quotas, and provides for "conservation" by taking land out of cultivation) has been controlled almost entirely by whites. Indeed it is incredible that as late as the end of 1968, no black was a regular member of a county conservation service committee. Blacks have had only token representation on either the state (when they held five of 58 positions in 1969) or community conservation service committees or the staffs which administer these programs. Except for employment in special places like the Data Processing Center and Commodity Office in Louisiana and the Eastern Photo Lab in North Carolina, very few blacks were employed by the service in the South. No blacks were employed above the GS-5 level in Alabama, Georgia, Kentucky, Mississippi, Oklahoma, South Carolina, Texas, or Virginia.

As of 1970, there were 232 black county conservation service employees from 2,007 total, only seven of whom (of 795) were above GS-5. There were no black service employees above GS-5 in Alabama, Florida, Georgia, Louisiana, Oklahoma, South Carolina, Tennessee, or Texas. No state outside the South had any black service employees at this level; indeed there was only one such black in any state outside the South (in Maryland). In 1970, there still were only two black county conservation service committeemen in the United States, and both of these were in Alabama (Office of Equal Opportunity, 1972, pp. 10–17).

The Cooperative Extension Service was established to help farmers improve their productivity by providing advice on management and technical aspects of farming, but the extension service also was racially segregated until 1964, has not had an effective outreach component, and therefore has done very little to help the poorest farmers improve their lot.

The extension service could not be completely impervious to the criticism of it, however; and during the 1960s it adopted a program designed to place paid and unpaid aides in some fifteen hundred communities to extend the same range of services to smaller farmers that it rendered to larger ones (*U.S. Organizational Manual*, 1972). Even though the aides program appears to have been moderately successful, it did not get under way until the number of small farmers had been greatly reduced. It also has had small amounts of resources relative to the total extension service program, and the range of programs participated in has been relatively small (*Proceedings*, 1972). However, this program has destroyed the prevailing myth in the agricultural "establishment" that low-income people lacked motivation to participate in USDA programs (Study Committee, 1968). Very few of those contacted by the aides program refused to participate in it. The programs helped train low-income farmers in record keeping, truck crop production, swine production, pasture improvement, beef cattle production, and home economics.

In addition to the aides program, there has been a modest increase in USDA research devoted to the problems of small farmers. Some of this research, particularly that of the Economic Research Service of the USDA, has been of high quality and very helpful in understanding the nature and dimensions of the problems of the rural poor. However, in the land grant college system, the amount of this research has been relatively small compared with that devoted to agricultural production.

Despite the growing national concern about rural problems (and urban problems originating in rural areas), only 289 of six thousand (less than 5 percent) scientific man-years spent on research in the land grant college complex in fiscal year 1969 could be classified as "people oriented" (Hightower, 1972, p. 14). Even these "people-oriented" projects often are more concerned with how entrepreneurs can make money than they are with how human needs can be met. For example, according to Hightower (p. 16), a major share of the rural housing research "has been directed not to those who live in them but to those who profit from the construction and maintenance of houses." Moreover, "other people-oriented projects tend to be irrelevant studies of characteristics, seemingly stemming more from curiosity than a desire to change conditions."

Some research useful to low-income farmers is being conducted in black land grant colleges, but these organizations receive infinitesimal parts of USDA research funds. In 1971, for example, black land grant colleges got only 0.5 percent of the $76.8 million allocated by the USDA for research in those sixteen states with black and white land grant colleges (Hightower, p. 20).

One reason for the character of the research done by the land grant college complex is the control of that system by interlocking forces representing the political, academic, and economic power structures. According to Hightower:

> Land grant policy is the product of a closed community. The administrators, academics, and scientists, along with USDA officials and corporate executives, have locked themselves into an inbred and even incestuous complex, and they are incapable of thinking beyond their self-interest and traditional concepts of agricultural research.

The Farmers Home Administration is supposed to make loans to enable small farmers to improve their homes, buy or expand farms, raise and market crops, buy machinery, or finance businesses which will improve their incomes. The administration also makes loans to farmers' cooperatives. Since it has concentrated its efforts in the geographic area of greatest rural poverty, a large proportion of the 48,000 Economic Opportunity Act loans made during the program's first four years were in the South. For example, the six largest recipients of such loans were Arkansas, Kentucky, Mississippi, North Carolina, Puerto Rico, and Texas; the states containing the largest number of cooperative loans were Arkansas, Louisiana, Minnesota, Mississippi, North Carolina, and Tennessee.

Since the administration was required by law to help those who could benefit from the loans, it helped whites more than it did blacks and the more affluent more than it did their poorer neighbors. For example, during the first four years, blacks (who constitute approximately 20 percent of the rural poor) received about 29 percent of the loans. But loans to blacks averaged only $1,755, as compared with $2,050 for others. Although blacks were about a third of all farmers in the South, and a much larger share of all poor farmers, between 1964 and 1967 they received only a fourth of all loans and a seventh of the funds (Beardwood, 1968).

The average family income the year before the loans were made was $2,082 for all recipients and $1,891 for farmers, and the average net income gain per family as a result of these loans was between $300 and $500 a year (Levitan, 1969).*

Although the characteristics of administration loan recipients might be a defense against "skimming" — since loans obviously went to people who were disadvantaged by urban standards — most blacks in the rural South would fall below the average income and education levels of those who got 'loans. In March 1965, for example, the median level of education of black male agricultural workers was 6.1 years, as compared with 9.4 years for whites. While 32 percent of Economic Opportunity Act loan recipients had a high school education or more, only 3.2 percent of nonwhite farm workers were in this category, and only 0.9 percent of nonwhite farmers and farm managers could meet this standard (Bureau of Labor Statistics, 1966, p. 204). And, as has been noted earlier, the average yearly incomes of black farmers in the South were a good bit less than the $1,891 for farmers who received opportunity loans. Moreover, the smaller average loans to blacks reflects, at least in part, the Farmers Home Administration's procedure of gearing the amount of the loan to the recipient's ability to use it. Since the more affluent, better educated borrowers could convince administration officials that they could make better use of the loans than their poorer, less educated neighbors, there obviously is an element of skimming inherent in its procedures. Although the approach used is imposed on the agency by law and is not necessarily due to its philosophy, administration officials nevertheless defend the procedure as maximizing the use of limited resources.

There also is conflicting evidence on the extent of racial discrimination in the administration of the Farmers Home Administration. Some officials point out that despite nondiscriminatory pronouncements from Washington, local administrators in the South reflect the racial prejudices of local political and agricultural leaders. In 1961, for example, there was not a single black among the seven thousand county committees which determine the eligibility of loan applicants. In 1969 there were 385 black county committeemen in the South, presumably because of the 1965 Farmers Home Administration's directive that counties where 20 percent of the farmers are black must have at least one black committeeman. In Alabama, there were thirty blacks among 183 administration committeemen in 1968, but none of the three-member com-

---

* The figures in this paragraph were from the Office of Economic Opportunity and Farmers Home Administration data in connection with Levitan's book.

mittccs had more than one black (Good, 1968). Despite black representation on the committees, the administration apparently had very
few blacks in staff positions. For example, there were only seven among
202 administration employees in Alabama in 1968 (Good, p. 21).

As of June 30, 1969, the Farmers Home Administration reported
170 black employees in the South (as compared with only 32 in 1965),
which was about 6 percent of its total southern employment. However,
a very large proportion of these 170 employees were employed at grades
GS-7 and above; in June 1969, only 28 were employed at GS-5 and
below. The largest category of employment for blacks in the administration was assistant county supervisors, of which there were 132 blacks;
there were five black county supervisors, eleven loan officers, and three
student trainees, but no loan chiefs or engineers.

Thus Farmers Home Administration has improved its black employment picture since 1965.* A survey of administration managers/-
supervisors during March 1971 found 199 black managers/supervisors
out of 3,972, or about 5 percent (Garnett, 1971, p. 6). In 1970, 217
of the Farmers Home Administration's 3,299 state and county employees
in the South were black (Office of Equal Opportunity, 1971, p. 50).

Conclusions

U.S. agricultural policy clearly has done very little historically for
black farmers in particular and small farmers in general. The machinery
to control and implement that policy — USDA and the land grant college system — apparently has been responsive primarily to the interests
of larger farmers, with minimal benefits to those with less land and capital. The prevailing philosophy has been that agricultural technology has
made small farmers obsolete. However, an examination of the evidence,
discussed below, shows this conclusion to be valid only in the sense that
the land and capital requirements for a one-man family farm have
increased, not that large corporate agribusinesses are more efficient
farmers than their smaller competitors.

There is some evidence that the agricultural "establishment" is
slowly changing its ways. The USDA moved in the late 1960s to hire
more blacks, but these still are grossly underrepresented on important
committees and on the payrolls of agricultural agencies which administer
the program. Similarly, the low-income loan and Cooperative Extension

* Employment statistics are from the director, Personnel Division, Farmers Home
Administration, Washington, D.C.

Service aides programs are steps in the right direction, but the loan program leads a precarious existence and probably will be cut out or greatly reduced by the Nixon administration. The aides program is logical and needed but has not been carefully evaluated. Moreover, much more could be done on research, demonstration, and extension work to low-income farmers, who apparently have been receptive to and have benefited from the aides program. The research and demonstration work of some groups concerned about small farmers could be a model for expanded government efforts. The Rural Development Act of 1972, to be administered by the USDA, contains a provision for research on the problems of small farmers (see chapter 3).

These reluctant moves in the right direction do not, however, solve the basic problem. Without really strong outright pressures, the USDA is not likely to respond to the needs of low-income farmers, because its basic philosophy is that small farmers are obsolete and have no real future in American agriculture. The prevailing attitude in the USDA probably was expressed by the deputy administrator of the Farmers Cooperative Service, who said (Washington *Post*, October 5, 1971):

> The low income farm problem is not personally my cup of tea. Our commercial co-ops are not exactly enthusiastic about them. They don't have much to offer except labor and it is less important today. These people were cotton choppers. They're tied up with idealism. The purpose of cooperatives is not to keep mass numbers in farming but to help those who remain. You can't go against market trends when everything else points to bigness.

The agricultural "establishment" has helped to make this philosophy a self-fulfilling prophecy.

THE FUTURE OF SMALL FARMERS

The migration from American agriculture undoubtedly will continue during the 1970s and 1980s, but some trends under way suggest that the rate of outmigration will be much less than it was during the 1950s and 1960s. These trends include rural industrialization and the declining relative income differentials of urban areas to be discussed later. Added to these must be the deteriorating quality of life in large metropolitan areas because of congestion and inadequate employment opportunities and declining tax bases as higher income whites migrate to the suburbs. There is also considerable evidence that increasing numbers of people prefer rural and small town to urban living (see chapter 5). As we shall see in the following chapters, nonfarm job opportunities are growing in rural areas, but the future opportunities for jobs in agriculture are not clear.

While the changing composition of agriculture is reducing the employment opportunities of migrants and seasonal farm workers, full-time employment opportunities in agriculture are rising and are likely to continue to do so as farm sizes increase and as farms become more capital intensive. Moreover, the rising agricultural-urban income ratio noted earlier probably reflects increasing economic viability of agricultural in comparison to nonagricultural sectors. In part, the reversal of the fifty-year depression in American agriculture might come because of the changing structure of American agriculture — especially the rapid increases in productivity — and partly because of increasing foreign demand for agricultural products (an underlying trend for years because of world food and fiber shortages, but first clearly obvious to the general public during 1972 and 1973 because of large foreign purchases of wheat and feed grains). Rising foreign demand results in part from agricultural production problems in other countries and in part from economic development, which has given them greater ability to pay for American agricultural imports.

While the outlook for agriculture and full-time agricultural workers is fairly bright, the prospects for small farmers are less clear. We have noted the long-run trend for small farmers to be displaced and for surviving farms to increase in size, as measured by land and capital requirements. The increasing profitability of agricultural activities suggested earlier could accelerate this trend. However, the strength of this trend, as well as the survival of small farms, depends upon economic policies as well as underlying economic realities. It would therefore be useful to determine the extent to which small farmers have been displaced by public policies and the extent to which their displacement has been due to their economic disadvantages as compared with larger farmers.

In addition to agricultural policy, small farmers have been displaced by technological changes that have greatly increased the minimum optimal acreage and capital requirements for even one- or two-man farms to sizes which are beyond the reach of most small farmers.

For example, a low-cost, one-man Illinois hog farm required over four hundred acres of land, produced 150 litters of pigs a year, required $200,000 total capital, and returned $23,000 to the operator for his labor and management (Van Arsdall and Elder, 1969). Similarly, a one-man irrigated cotton farm in Texas included 440 acres (140 acres of which were in cotton) and capital requirements of nearly $300,000 and returned $20,000 to the operator (Davis and Madden, 1965). A southern farm management regional research project conducted by the USDA and the land grant universities involved 121 farm resource situations in the South and, according to Sundquist (1971, p. 7),

> . . . generally show[ed] that in order to realize an annual farm operator income of $5,000 the smallest farm in the Southeast would have to be over 100 acres and range up to 900 acres, depending on commodity prices, location, and soil productivity. The dollar investment required ranged from some $20,000 to over $100,000.

The requisite land sizes and capital requirements in the Southwest were higher. Clearly, therefore, the optimal-size farm, which has been made larger by advancing technology and capital requirements, is likely to be beyond the reach of most marginal farmers.

If we attempt to assess the future of small farmers, it would be useful to distinguish the extent to which large farmers have increased their share of total farm sales because of economic advantages or the extent to which their advantages are due to preferential treatment under U.S. agricultural and tax policies. Their agricultural policy advantage is fairly clear. However, large nonagricultural businesses also have tax advantages in their farm operations. They can use farm costs to reduce nonfarm income and pay only capital gains rather than higher income taxes on the sale of land. These nonagricultural enterprises compete with farm operators who do not have these tax advantages.

But these are policies that can be changed. Are there economic advantages inherent in the size of large farms? This is a very difficult question to answer technically, because we cannot adequately control for all things other than size. Moreover, the economic theory applicable to this question is of little value because we are not concerned with economies of scale — where all factors of production are varied simultaneously, which rarely if ever happens in the real world — but with economies of size, where factors vary at different rates.

Agricultural economists have used three broad types of approaches to analyze the economies of size question:

(1) Synthetic farms, where models are used to approximate the influence of economies of scale (Brewster, 1954; Bressler, 1945, pp. 526–93; Madden, 1967). Technical coefficients are derived from a variety of sources, including experimental data, model farms, and manufacturers' performance data.

(2) Cross-sectional analysis of actual farm record data, where costs and returns from farms of different sizes are analyzed, usually by regression or analysis of variance, to determine the relationship between production costs and size.

(3) Analysis of the secular trend in the size distribution of farms over time, using census or other survey data. As noted earlier, these data show large farms to be increasing their share of farm sales relative to smaller ones.

Size may be measured in terms of acreage, labor used, gross income, net income, or value added. However, most studies have been in terms of labor, because this is a more homogeneous and measurable input.

A number of general conclusions have been reached by the "synthetic" studies of the economies of farm size:

(1) In terms of costs per unit of output, most of the economies of size can be obtained by a one- or two-man, fully mechanized farm (Sundquist, 1971).

(2) Even though unit costs may reach their low point within the size range of one- or two-man units, there is little tendency for costs to rise as farm sizes increase, providing an incentive for farms to increase total profits through larger outputs.

However, some studies have found rising costs beyond certain sizes *in terms of acreage*. For example a synthetic analysis of cash-crop farms in Yolo County, California, producing a variety of crops found that all economies of size were produced at six hundred to eight hundred acres and that firms over fourteen hundred acres experienced rising average costs (Dean and Carter, 1960).

The cross-sectional studies usually are derived from individual census records, supplemented with survey information. A study of seven cotton and tobacco farms in the South using this method found that only two large cotton farms (one in the Mississippi Delta and the other in the Texas high plains, with capital investments of $324,593 and $154,197, respectively) had returns comparable to alternative nonfarm employments of labor and capital (Economic Research Service, October 1967).

The cross-sectional studies have a number of limitations in providing insight into the economies of farm size. In the first place, the technique used limits the amount of data that can be analyzed. Moreover, studies of actual farm operations reveal considerable variation in efficiency from case to case. The averages fitted to these data therefore are not likely to provide much insight into the optimal farm size. The census studies provide more information, but they too fail to abstract from policy factors. Some studies have attempted to control for the inherent defects in cross-sectional data and differences in degree of plant utilization by using composite firm budgets (Madden, 1967, pp. 27–28).

Thus none of those three approaches is entirely satisfactory. If it were based on empirically derived assumptions, the synthetic approach would provide valuable insights, but most of these studies employ static, pure competition assumptions and assume constant product and factor prices. These studies are limited because they commonly assume away or ignore the diseconomies resulting from management problems in large-scale firms.

Some Theoretical Aspects of Economies of Farm Size

Although the neoclassical theory of economies of scale provides few empirically testable insights into the cost advantages of different sized farms, empirical work by some agricultural economists provides some generalizations. The writer has found the work of Madden and Partenheimer (1972) to be particularly helpful, but theoretical insights also are provided by the empirical work of others.

The theory of fixed assets, which postulates that firms view assets as fixed so long as marginal value product (the contribution to total revenue from the sale of additional output) is less than replacement cost and greater than salvage value, helps to explain why costs do not necessarily increase with size. If an operator's labor has zero salvageable value (opportunity cost) because of limited nonfarm opportunities, the operator will view labor as a fixed cost, but his marginal value product in farming is above zero (or whatever amount he considers his opportunity cost to be) but still below its replacement cost (the cost of hiring an additional worker). As a consequence, this farmer might remain in farming the rest of his life, even though his revenue did not cover total costs but was greater than variable costs.

Economic theory often assumes resources to be divisible and fully utilized. However, resources often are discrete and not fully utilized, although divisibility could be approximated if all resources could be hired on a custom or contract basis. Larger farms might have an advantage in fully using large discrete resources, but this might be offset by custom farming or the perfection of smaller machines more adaptable to small farm conditions. For example, synthetic studies of crop farms and crop-livestock farms in Iowa found two-man farms to have some advantage over one-man operations. However, when custom hiring of some farm operations was introduced into the analysis, the smaller farm's cost curves dropped by 25 percent, making them nearly as efficient as the two-man farm (Heady and Kreng, 1962; Ihnen and Heady, 1964).

Since these studies examined only one- and two-man operations, they do not provide information on a range of farm sizes, but they do indicate that smaller farms could lower their costs appreciably by such practices as custom hiring of activities requiring expensive machinery. Larger farms might have diseconomies in the purchase of such machinery if they could not keep it fully occupied.

Coordination and uncertainty in economic operations require some compensation or cost. However, the relationship between uncertainty and coordination and farm size is not clear. Some aspects of large farm operations clearly increase uncertainty and coordination, particularly lack of resource uniformity and the spatial dispersion of resources. With respect to the former, uncertainties for large farms are increased by different soil types, product outputs, and qualities of labor inputs. Coordination problems are also created when large farms have different kinds of operations under way at some distance from each other. Large farms can compensate for the disadvantages of uncertainty and coordination, but they must incur costs (more expensive management, transportation, and communication equipment) in order to do so.

Financial advantages of large farms probably outweigh disadvantages. With respect to taxes, large firms might have disadvantages from higher income and inheritance tax brackets. Although large integrated farms might also have the advantage of being able to shift costs to their nonfarm operations, this advantage has nothing to do with economies of farm size. Large farms also have economies in large-scale purchases, but they have diseconomies in having to internalize some costs (roads, social overhead) that are borne by the public for smaller farms. Thus while large farms have financial advantages and disadvantages, the advantages probably far outweigh the disadvantages.

Large farms probably have net disadvantages in *labor utilization*. Large farmers requiring considerable labor at harvest or other times when crops or livestock require attention suffer losses if they are unable to get adequate supplies at the proper time. Moreover, large farms must hire managers and pay prevailing wages, which probably are above the opportunity cost of labor to the family farm. Large farmers have been able to minimize their risks from uncertain labor supplies by shifting them to workers, who bear the main costs (in the form of low wages, unemployment, and underemployment) for the excess supplies of labor farm interests have encouraged in order to meet peak labor demands and keep wages down. However, this advantage might be short-lived, because farm populations are declining, alternative rural nonfarm employment opportunities have reduced agricultural labor supplies, and pressures are building from agricultural workers' organizations and the public to shift some of the costs of maintaining peak labor supplies from agricultural workers to employers through collective bargaining, the extension of social benefits to agricultural workers, and measures to restrict foreign labor competition. Family workers probably also have more interest in the quality of work they do than the workers hired by agribusinesses, particularly when those hired are casual workers with limited attachments to particular employers.

Much of the literature on economies of farm size not only ignores managerial and coordination costs but also is unrealistic in assuming that small farmers depend entirely on farm income. As we saw earlier, there is a growing trend for farmers to work in nonfarm jobs; indeed, on the average, farm operators now get more of their income from nonfarm activities, including farm work for wages, than they do from farming. Therefore, even if small farms were not as efficient as large ones, they could compete so long as they could earn at least the opportunity costs of their total family labor and nonlabor resources, not just that part devoted to farming. To these earnings must be added whatever psychic income small farmers derive from leading the kind of life they prefer.

Although on balance U.S. agricultural policy clearly benefits larger farmers more than smaller ones, this factor also has had differential results. Larger farmers benefit primarily because most commodity payments are on the basis of acreage, poundage, or some other measure of volume. However, payments not based on volume (like the diversion payments for feed grains) were much less regressive than the commodity programs (Bonnen, 1968); and also some noncommodity programs tended to be progressive in the sense that they helped smaller farmers more than larger ones (McKee and Day, 1968). Similarly, tobacco allotments, which were attached to the land before 1971, making it difficult for larger farmers to buy up the allotments of smaller operators without also buying the land, helped smaller farmers survive (Economic Research Service, 1969). However, the tobacco program was changed in 1971 to make it possible to detach allotments from the land so long as they were kept in the same county, making greater consolidation possible.

Are Family Farms Disappearing?

There has been some controversy in recent years over whether or not family farms are increasing or decreasing compared to large or corporate farms. The position of USDA is that family farms, "those using predominately family labor, make up 95 percent of all farms and produce 65 percent of all farm products sold in the U.S. Although these percentages have fluctuated slightly, they have been substantially the same for the last 30 years, despite the decline in total farm numbers" (Nikolitch, February 1972, p. 15). This conclusion is based upon a special Census of Agriculture study in which family farms were defined as those in which a majority of the work was done by the farm operator and his family, and nonfamily farms were those where hired labor did more than half the work.

USDA found that family farms constituted 95 percent of all farms in 1949, 1959, 1964, and 1969, but accounted for the following proportions of sales in these years: 1949, 63 percent; 1959, 70 percent; 1964, 65 percent; and 1969, 62 percent. It also uses land tenure data from the Census of Agriculture to support its argument that family farms predominate. These data show the following proportions of farms owned by and land cultivated by owner-operators (Moyer *et al.*, June 1969, p. 14; U.S. Census of Agriculture, 1972):

Year	Percentage of Farms	Percentage of Land
1900	63.7%	63.3%
1920	60.9	66.7
1940	60.7	64.3
1964	82.4	76.7
1969	88.1	86.9

USDA also contends that corporate farms are not a significant force in U.S. agriculture. According to Secretary of Agriculture Butz, "Less than one percent of our total farms are corporate farms, and about six out of seven (89 percent) of these are family corporation farms. They are really family farms" (*Wisconsin Agriculturist*, January 8, 1972, p. 12, cited by Rodefeld, 1973, p. 10). However, these figures and conclusions have been challenged by Rodefeld who shows: first, USDA's figures on family farms are misleading because of changing definitions. In 1949, for example, plantations were counted as single units and presumably "nonfamily" farms; in 1959, sharecroppers were counted as independent family farms. This made it appear that nonfamily farms (plantations) were disappearing and family farms (sharecroppers) were growing. "If multiple-unit operations had been included for the years 1959, 1964, and 1969, then other than family farms would have consistently accounted for an increasing proportion of all farm sales from 1949 to 1969." In addition, "if this had been done, then family sized farms at the present time would account for a good deal less than the 62 percent of all farm sales" (Rodefeld, p. 15).

Second, USDA's aggregate data conceal the following regional variations in control of farms and sales by nonfamily farms:

Region	Percentage of Farms	Percentage of Sales
Pacific	13%	71%
Southeastern	6	56
Mountain	9	54
Delta	8	51
New England	11	49
Southern plains	6	45
Lake states	2	14
Corn belt	2	13
Northern plains	2	18
Appalachia	4	27

Thus in most of the regions, except for the Midwest, nonfamily farms controlled large percentages of total farm sales, even though they accounted for relatively few farms. Moreover, in each of USDA's eleven regions, sales accounted for by family-size farms declined between 1959 and 1964. Control of various crops by nonfamily farms was as follows:

Crop	Percentage of Farms	Percentage of Sales
Vegetables	17%	85%
Fruits and nuts	17	71
Other field crops	20	70
Cotton	10	53
Poultry	8	43
Other livestock	3	31
General	5	30
Dairy	6	23
Tobacco	3	18
Cash grain	3	15

Third, the classification of farms by tenant (owner operated) gives misleading results because (a) we do not know the extent to which owners own their land and nonland assets, and (b) the definition of farm operator was changed between 1964 and 1969 for "a person . . . either doing the work himself or directly supervising the work" to "the person in charge of the farm or ranch operation." This definition made it possible to classify in 1969 as "owners" people who were previously classified as hired managers and absentee owners.

And finally, USDA's definition of corporate farm also is misleading. Corporations are defined as only those corporations with ten or more stockholders. However, this definition probably omits most farm corporations. Using a structural definition of corporate farms (large acreage or sales-wise absentee owners, hired managers, and hired workers), Rodefeld found as the basis of studies in Wisconsin "approximately 75 percent of all structurally defined, legally incorporated 'corporate' farms were owned by an individual, family, or small groups of individuals. None of these 'corporate' farms would have been included in the USDA's 'corporate' farm category" (p. 21). His findings (Table 2-5) show owner-operated, family-size farms to have ceased accounting for a majority of farm sales between 1959 and 1964, but to have accounted for more than three-fourths of all farms. However, they also show the larger-than-family farms to be gaining in sales relative to family farms.

TABLE 2-5

Reclassification of Farms According to Rodefeld
(Millions)

Category	Percentage of Farms		Percentage of Change 1959–64	Percentage of All Sales		Percentage of Change 1959–64
	1959	1964		1959	1969	
All farms	100.0%	100.0%	−14.7%	100.0%	100.0%	15.5%
Owner operated family sized	76.0	78.6	−11.9	50.1	49.3	11.9
Nonowner operated, family sized (tenant)	19.5	16.5	−27.7	19.5	15.3	− 9.1
Owner operated, larger than family sized	3.8	3.9	−12.2	23.7	25.4	23.8
Nonowner operated, larger than family sized	0.7	1.0	23.1	6.7	10.0	73.5

Conclusions

To return to our original question — what has caused the displacement of small farmers in the United States? The answer is not easy to give because the causes are not clear. We do know that technology has increased the minimum size of the optimal sized farm. If small farmers could acquire the necessary human and physical capital, many of them presumably could compete effectively with larger agribusinesses, especially those which are engaged exclusively in agriculture, because there apparently are few if any across-the-board cost advantages for large farms. However, larger capital requirements for the smallest optimal sized farm, the advantages of U.S. agricultural policy, land speculation, and volume clearly give larger farmers an increasing share of the market. Volume is important in marketing agricultural products because bargaining power in dealing with buyers often is directly proportional to the control of supplies.

Nevertheless, public policies could be taken to help smaller farmers and moderate or even halt their decline. These measures include shifting some public expenditures from larger to smaller farmers; research on inexpensive machinery that could be employed on smaller acreages; research on crops and techniques that would make it possible for smaller, labor-intensive farms to maximize the returns to their resources; encouraging cooperatives and other organizations to represent the interests of low-income farmers and rural workers; and the provision of alternate forms of income in rural areas through industrialization, manpower programs, and public employment. Some form of income maintenance, like that contemplated by several welfare reform proposals, probably would stimulate small-scale farming as supplementary income.

Some private organizations, such as the National Sharecroppers Fund, the Federation of Southern Cooperatives, and some black colleges, have research and demonstration programs on the problems of small farmers which could serve as models for expanded public programs. Alternatively, public funds could be used to support such efforts as these. The National Sharecroppers Fund has experimented with organic farming on an experimental farm in North Carolina to see if migrants can be trained in organic farming and one skill, like welding, which would be useful for farm and nonfarm employment. These experiments indicate that earnings of $600 per acre can be realized from organic vegetables without processing and as much as $3,000 per acre if vegetables are processed cooperatively. In addition to the experimental farm, the National Sharecroppers Fund has been instrumental in forming a number of rural cooperatives.

PROBLEMS OF MIGRANT WORKERS

The most disadvantaged group of agricultural workers in the United States is generally regarded to be migrants who travel from place to place following the crops. The problems of these workers are well known and therefore need only to be summarized here. In 1969, it was reported that the 172,000 migratory workers who were employed more than 25 days at farm work averaged $1,937 for 152 days of farm and nonfarm work (*Manpower Report*, 1971, p. 123). In 1970, migrants earned $1,930 for 88 days of farm work and $777 for 45 days of nonfarm work, or $2,707 (McElroy, 1971).

Besides low wages, migrants have suffered from discrimination against them in their home areas and the places where they work. Not only have they been considered to be low-status workers because of the nature of their jobs, many have suffered additional problems because they are blacks, chicanos, or other minorities. Chicanos suffer from competition from hundreds of thousands, if not millions, of legal and illegal entrants from Mexico. Indeed many chicanos apparently have entered the migrant stream because they could not compete for jobs with Mexican nationals (Briggs, 1973). But the migrants' main problems are associated with the fact that they must move from place to place in order to find work. Their work is therefore intermittent, and they have difficulty obtaining services and living conditions less mobile people take for granted. As former Assistant Secretary of Labor for Manpower Malcolm Lovell reported to the Subcommittee on Agricultural Labor of the House Committee on Education and Labor, "At the heart of the migrants' problems is the fact that our social and political institutions are designed to serve a stable population and have not exhibited the capacity to meet the special needs of people on the move" (June 30, 1971).

As a consequence of their mobility, migrants develop what Coles (1969, p. 14), a Harvard psychiatrist, calls a "migrant subculture," characterized by social isolation.

> The extreme poverty, the cultural deprivation and social fragmentation, in sum the uprootedness which characterizes their lives, falls not suddenly upon them (as it does upon the observer who tries to comprehend their manner of survival) but is a constant fact of life from birth to death, summoning, therefore, a whole life style, a full range of adaptive maneuvers.

These adaptive maneuvers include family cohesion and suspicion of outsiders. The migrant subculture includes deteriorating health at an early stage in young adults and the rapid maturity of children which causes them to become "adults" between ages ten and twelve. Migrants may respond to these stresses by heavy drinking and "nasty and violent" dispositions. The psychological effect of this existence is: ". . . a tendency to feel not only weak and hard pressed, but responsible for that fate" (Coles, 1969, p. 17).

It is clear that migrants continue to "follow the crops" out of necessity and lack of alternatives rather than by choice. For example, a study of migrants in Michigan found that 77 percent of the migrants would leave farm work if they could, and only 5 percent of them wanted their children to become farm laborers (Santos, 1971).

Remedies

The remedies for the migrant laborers' conditions seem fairly obvious. To some extent, of course, migrants have all of the problems of other rural workers, so the remedies discussed elsewhere in this volume would benefit them. However, migrants have special problems because of their migratory existence. Their special needs include: reducing the irregularity of their employment, special educational needs for children in motion, adequate housing and health facilities, legal aid, and programs to help them "settle out" of the migrant stream.

Many people concerned with the problems of migrants are persuaded that the only real solution to the migrants' problems is to eliminate migrancy as a way of life. This can be done through increasing the use of local workers to meet seasonal agricultural needs. While growers have argued that local manpower could not be found for "stoop" labor in the fields, the results following the termination of the bracero program in 1964 suggest that local labor supplies were larger than many supposed. But other sources of income also will be required for seasonal workers who cannot make a living entirely from local seasonal work in agriculture.

As noted earlier, to some extent labor market developments are reducing the numbers of migrants. The most important cause of declining demand for migrants is mechanization. However, the introduction of machinery is stimulated by technological innovations, rising labor costs, and uncertain supplies of labor, all of which give growers incentives to substitute machinery for labor. A major source of rising labor costs, according to growers, has been rising housing costs due to stringent housing requirements by the federal government (which adopted minimum housing standards in July 1967) and by many states with large numbers of migrants. Indeed, many growers and their representatives feel that these and other demands on behalf of the migrants create serious problems for farmers (Sullivan, 1971).

Rising labor costs also have resulted from the cumulative effects of successive increases in minimum wages between 1966 and 1969, to be discussed later.

Migrant Programs

A number of programs have been adopted to help migrants. One of the earliest of these was the Annual Worker Plan started in 1954. This plan was designed to coordinate the demand and supply for migrant labor and thereby reduce the time between jobs. The employment service agencies in the supply states, mainly Texas and Florida, determine the numbers of migrants available, and the agencies in the demand states determine the amount of labor needed. From this information, an agricultural worker schedule is prepared as an itinerary for a migratory crew or family. However, the number of groups using the plan has declined since 1967–69, primarily because of mechanization and changing production techniques ("Annual Worker Plan," 1971, p. 26). According to the Texas Good Neighbor Commission's 1970 annual report, the plan has also been in trouble since 1967 because employers who were not in compliance with the new housing regulations were not allowed to use the plan.

> The failure of many employers to comply with the new [housing] standards has almost blown the Plan out of the window. . . . [The] decreases are slowing somewhat but this is of little solace when we survey the damage already done to our system of job placement; the mutual commitment is badly weakened (p. 3 of summary).

Another project designed to test new methods for dealing with migrant problems was the Manpower Administration's migrant demonstration project started in ten states in 1969. The purpose of this project was to "explore ways to help migrants either leave the migrant stream or, if they wanted to remain in it, to get any supportive assistance they needed" (Marshall, 1971, p. 11). The project made it possible for local employment offices to hire rural outreach interviewers to work with migrants. This approach was in keeping with the Labor Department's attempt to change its rural manpower approach from being a supplier of labor to employers to being more responsive to the needs of workers. The plan called for testing various ways to help migrants through a demonstration project involving 705 families selected in Texas by the rural outreach interviewers. However, this plan was abandoned because many of the migrants could not be located and other families were selected in order to carry out the project. The original plan also failed because the U.S. Employment Service failed to coordinate with local Office of Economic Opportunity migrant projects in soliciting assistance.

Because of defects in the project design and the absence of a careful evaluation, it is difficult to know what effect the migrant demonstration project actually had. The best feature of the project apparently was the use of outreach interviewers as bridges between local employment offices and migrants.

> The [rural outreach interviewers] played a key role in the project and needed dedication and a broad background. They had to be sensitive to migrant views, know local resources, be able to deal skillfully with a variety of agencies, be willing to work odd and long hours, and be able to exert pressure in meeting migrant needs (Marshall, p. 12).

The interviewers were particularly useful in helping migrants find housing, health facilities, and jobs, in providing much other assistance to workers making the transition from the migrant stream, or in improving their conditions in it. The rural outreach interviewers apparently accomplished a great deal in making manpower, welfare, and education agencies more responsive to the migrant's needs. After two years, however, the program was discontinued, and the states were supposed to build services to migrants into their regular procedures (Cronemeyer, 1972, p. 9).

Although statistics are not available, there is agreement that the project did not settle many migrants out of the stream. Apparently, the project encountered a number of obstacles to carrying out its objectives, including: considerable variation in effectiveness of the rural outreach interviewers; the selection of too large and unwieldy a sample at the outset; the reluctance of consumer states to build services to settle out migrants, whom many considered to be undesirable "outsiders"; and basic defects in selecting goals which were too broad and in not carefully selecting target areas for the migrants. A basic problem seems to have been that the employment services and other agencies in labor-consumer states were not interested in rendering services to "Texas Mexicans."

After the first year, a Texas authority reported that "all we have really learned from this project is that the migrants' problems and difficulties are virtually the same as we have known them to be for years, and that attempting to obtain coordination and cooperation on a large, interstate scale is infinitely more complex than was originally presumed."

In 1971, the U.S. Department of Labor announced a new program, the National Migrant Worker Plan, to help workers make the transition from migrant agriculture to stable nonagricultural employment. The plan's program grew out of the migrant experiments and demonstration project and was designed to settle out 5,800 migrants the first year. The program's main strategy was to provide training and job development in the home base area and programs to settle people out of the migrant stream. Mobility facilitation units coordinate services from central locations along the migratory stream. The manpower specialists attached to these units were to provide job development, basic education, occupational counseling, supplementary training, and financial assistance. Other agencies also were to provide services of various kinds.

Instead of recruiting in Texas, as the migrant experiment and demonstration project attempted to do, the National Migrant Worker Plan contacts people in the migrant stream and encourages them to settle outside it.

This project should encounter less resistance than former plans to help migrants. For one thing, the demand for migrants is declining, so there should be much less grower opposition than in former years. Moreover, the sharp decline in job opportunities for migrants in many areas during 1970 and 1971 has made these workers desperate for programs to provide new jobs. As noted earlier, most migrants seem to have very little attachment to this work; they have remained in it out of necessity rather than from any personal attachment to it.

Migrant Education

There are a number of other special projects for migrants which should be mentioned. One of these is the Texas migrant education program launched in 1962. Beginning with three thousand students in the Rio Grande Valley in 1963, this program expanded to include 55,000 students in 99 districts in 1970 and 1971. The basic objective of the project is to meet the special education needs of migrants. Special programs to accomplish this include preschool training to prepare five-year-olds for the first grade, programs to gear the school year to the special needs of migrants, summer school and enrichment programs, provision of special materials and teachers, cooperation with other states in the migrant streams, and bilingual education.

Federal funds for migrant education are available under Title I of the Elementary and Secondary Education Act of 1965. During 1967, the first full year of operation under the "migrant amendment" to Title I, the federal government awarded $9.5 million to 44 states; this amount rose to $37.7 million in 1968. In addition, the U.S. Office of Education has allotted funds for migrants under other titles. Moreover, the Office of Economic Opportunity launched programs for migrants which provided day care, adult education, a compensatory education program, a high school equivalency program, and education and consulting to project directors. The Office of Education also has funded a uniform migrant student record transfer system to facilitate the transfer of migrant student records through a computerized system with three hundred terminals.

The education of migrant children remains a controversial question. Migrants and their spokesmen are very critical of the program, for which $97 million was appropriated the first three years. For example, the National Committee on the Education of Migrant Children reported in 1971 that the program "had not dented indifference to and neglect of migrants on the part of cities and states." Moreover, the writer's conversations with Texas education officials suggest that the migrant education project has done very little, other than changing school schedules, to gear education to the value systems and experiences of migrant children.

Migrant Health

The special health needs of migrants led to the passage of the Migrant Health Act of 1962, amended in 1970 to cover all seasonal farm workers, which authorized the Public Health Service to work with interested public and voluntary groups to upgrade health services available to migrants. This program at first had an annual appropriations ceiling of $3 million for three years, which was cut in 1969, but it was extended in 1970 for three years with annual appropriations of $20 million in 1970, $25 million in 1971, and $30 million in 1972. At first this program was hampered by lack of knowledge and indifference by migrants, resistance from the health establishment, community rejection, inadequate resources, and difficulties involved in administering health care to a mobile population. However, the program apparently has caught on and has become a continuing health service for seasonal farm workers. There are, for example, 33 clinics operating under this program in Texas.

Rural Legal Assistance

Because they lacked effective organizations to represent them before the 1960s, the rural poor were able to do very little to change their conditions. However, during the 1960s, a number of organizations emerged to join established groups like the National Sharecroppers Fund and the American Civil Liberties Union in performing advocacy functions. The rural poor often had serious needs for legal assistance to protect their property and civil rights, which were sometimes encroached on by more affluent people who could use the law to their advantage. During the 1960s, the Office of Economic Opportunity's legal services projects did much to correct specific abuses and to bring the plight of the rural poor to the nation's attention. Other Office of Economic Opportunity-funded organizations have also performed this function.

One important area where legal assistance has helped migrants has been in protecting their right to have visitors in labor camps. In many areas, growers have refused to permit access to the camps, even to family and friends, but especially to poverty workers, lawyers, and union organizers. Visitors have apparently been barred in part because the growers have ignored child labor, minimum wage, housing, and other laws and did not want reporters writing stories about camp conditions. In a landmark 1971 case instigated by the Migrant Legal Action Program, Inc., of Washington, D.C., a federal district judge ordered a Michigan grower to grant free access to a migrant labor camp and assessed damages of $4,500 against him for interfering with visits to a family in his camp (New York *Times,* October 4, 1971).

Legal assistance workers have also done much to help the rural poor qualify for welfare and other public programs. They have performed legal services in connection with the formation of various legal organizations through which the rural poor seek to help themselves, have brought action to prevent harassment by public officials, and have sued various government agencies, including the Rural Manpower Service of the Department of Labor, to make those agencies more responsive to the needs of workers. A 1971 suit by a number of migrants and their legal representatives accused the Farm Labor Service (now the Rural Manpower Service) of "bureaucratic malfeasance," of being "grower-staffed and oriented," and of exploiting migrant farmworkers through discriminatory acts in violation of the Wagner-Peyser Act and Title VI of the Civil Rights Act (New York *Times*, August 3, 1971). Former Assistant Secretary of Labor Malcolm Lovell considered these charges to be very serious and ordered a thorough investigation. (See "Rural Manpower Service" in chapter 4 for further discussion of this case.)

The California Rural Legal Assistance Agency antagonized Governor Ronald Reagan and other officials by such actions as successfully challenging medical care budget cuts in California, forcing the Department of Agriculture to extend the food stamp program to 58 counties that had refused to participate, filing suit against the Secretary of Labor for not enforcing his own ban of Mexican workers, and forcing removal of an injunction against the payment of $1.65 an hour for women workers, which forced growers to pay the higher rate and $800,000 in back wages.

These activities have elicited considerable opposition from growers, public officials, and other established groups in rural areas. Those who participated in the legal assistance projects were accused of "stirring up trouble" and acting arrogantly. Local authorities were particularly concerned about efforts on the migrants' behalf to gain access to public education, housing, welfare, and other programs. Local leaders also were concerned about the challenge to their economic and political control from those who represented the rural poor.

Conclusions on Migrants

Thus considerable attention has been devoted to the problems of migrants, and the magnitude of this problem is being diminished by the steady decline in the demand for seasonal agricultural workers. However, some migrant representatives dispute the Labor Department's figures. In any event, it probably is an exaggeration to consider migrants the most disadvantaged group in rural America. Their plight is desperate because of declining demand and because their mobile nature creates special problems for them.

But there are many other workers in the United States, especially in the deep South, who have lower incomes and equally serious problems. Because they are in motion and therefore visible, migrants have caught public attention, although Senator Walter Mondale, chairman of the Senate Subcommittee on Migratory Labor, is correct in arguing that migrants have benefited relatively little from that attention, despite many programs designed to help them (New York *Times*, March 22, 1971). The nonmigrant poor black, white, and brown agricultural workers are less visible, but their problems are at least as bad. Moreover, there are many more of these workers than there are migrants.

Mexican Workers

As noted earlier, one of the problems confronting rural workers in the Southwest has been the competition they face from legal and illegal entrants from Mexico. This problem has been exacerbated in recent years by the location of plants along the Mexican side of the border to assemble goods to be sold in the United States. A special provision of the U.S. tariff code makes it possible for these goods to be shipped back into the United States tariff free, except for the increase in their value while in Mexico, which is equal to the small amount of wages paid to Mexicans. These plants apparently attract many more workers to the border than they can provide jobs for. Although we know very little about the extent of this problem, many of these excess workers have joined the large numbers who have crossed the border every year either as commuters or illegal aliens.

Commuters are persons who live in Mexico but work in the United States; they are technically immigrants, but they can live where they please. They are free to come and go as they please so long as no absence from the United States exceeds one year or they do not become unemployed for over six months. The Texas Good Neighbor Commission reported in 1970 that there are 702,000 Mexican green carders, 80 percent of whom are concentrated in Texas and California. At the end of May 1969, of these green carders, 47,315 Mexican alien commuters were identified, 88 percent of whom worked in Texas and California — 22,263 in Texas and 19,423 in California (Hennessy, 1969, pp. 67–70). There were, in addition, innumerable illegal entrants — 277,377 Mexicans were apprehended and deported in 1970.

These Mexican workers create serious problems for rural workers in the Southwest, whose wages are depressed by their presence. Moreover, the organization of unions and the adoption of other measures to improve the workers' lot are dissipated by large supplies of workers crossing the border. The chief victims of this competition from people who have American wages and Mexican living costs are chicanos who compete most directly with them. As with other powerless groups, chicanos have had little influence on policies to curb commuters and illegal entrants.

REFERENCES

Agricultural Economics Reports, nos. 120, 148, 164, 218. Washington, D.C.: U.S. Department of Agriculture, Economic Research Service. 1967–69 and 1971.

"Annual Worker Plan in 1970." *Rural Manpower Developments* (September-October 1971).

Arkansas Agriculture Experiment Station, Fayetteville, Arkansas. *Cotton: Supply, Demand, and Resource Use.* Southern Cooperative Series Bulletin No. 110. November 1966.

Baldwin, Sidney. *Poverty and Politics.* Chapel Hill: University of North Carolina Press. 1968.

Beale, Calvin. "Discussion." Paper prepared for *Human Resource Development in the Rural South.* Austin: University of Texas, Center for the Study of Human Resources. 1971. Final report to the Office of Economic Opportunity. Mimeographed.

——————. "Rural-Urban Migration of Blacks: Past and Future." *American Economic Review* (May 1971).

Beardwood, Roger. "Southern Roots of Urban Crisis." *Fortune* (August 1968).

Benedict, Murray A. *Farm Policies of the United States, 1790–1950.* New York: The Twentieth Century Fund. 1953.

Bishop, C. E. "Dimensions of the Farm Labor Problem." In *Farm Labor in the United States.* Edited by C. E. Bishop. New York: Columbia University Press. 1967.

——————. "Economic Aspects of Changes in the Farm Labor Force." In *Labor Mobility and the Population in Agriculture.* Ames: Iowa State University, Center for Agricultural and Economic Adjustment. 1961.

Blau, Peter M.; and Duncan, Otis D. "Farm Backgrounds and Occupational Achievement." In *The American Occupational Structure.* New York: John Wiley & Sons, Inc. 1967.

Bonnen, James. "The Distribution of Benefits from Selected U.S. Farm Programs." In President's National Advisory Committee on Rural Poverty, *Rural Poverty in the United States.* Washington, D.C.: U.S. Government Printing Office. 1968.

Bressler, Raymond G. "Research Determination of Economies of Scale." *Journal of Farm Economics* (August 1945), vol. 27, no. 3.

Brewster, John M. *Comparative Economies of Different Types of Cottonseed Oil Mills and Their Effect on Oil Supplies, Prices, and Returns to Growers.* Marketing Research Report No. 54. Washington, D.C.: U.S. Department of Agriculture. 1954.

Briggs, Vernon M., Jr. *Chicanos and Rural Poverty.* Baltimore: The Johns Hopkins Press. 1973.

Bureau of Labor Statistics. *The Negroes in the United States.* Bulletin No. 1511. Washington, D.C.: U.S. Department of Agriculture. June 1966.

Changes in Farm Production and Efficiency. Washington, D.C.: U.S. Department of Agriculture. 1969.

—————: *A Summary Report.* Washington, D.C.: U.S. Department of Agriculture. June 1967.

Coles, Robert. *Migrants, Sharecroppers, Mountaineers.* Boston: Little, Brown and Company. 1971.

—————. "Statement to Subcommittee on Migratory Labor." In *The Migratory Farm Labor Problem in the United States.* Washington, D.C.: U.S. Government Printing Office. 1969.

Conrad, David E. *The Forgotten Farmers.* Urbana: The University of Illinois Press. 1965.

Cronemeyer, Cora S. "New Ways of Helping Migrants." *Rural Manpower* (March 1972).

Davis, Robert; and Madden, J. Patrick. *Economies of Size on Irrigated Cotton Farms.* Texas Agricultural Experiment Station Bulletin No. 1037. June 1965.

Dean, Gerald W.; and Carter, Harold O. *Cost-Size Relationships for Cash Crop Farms in Yolo County, California.* Agricultural Economics Report No. 238. Agricultural Experiment Station. Giannini Foundation. 1960.

Economic Research Service. *Farm Costs and Returns: Commercial Farms by Type, Size, and Location.* Agricultural Information Bulletin No. 230. Washington, D.C.: U.S. Department of Agriculture. October 1967.

—————. *Potential Mechanization in the Flue-Cured Tobacco Industry.* Agricultural Economics Report No. 169. Washington, D.C.: U.S. Department of Agriculture. 1969.

—————. *The Farm Income Situation.* Washington, D.C.: U.S. Department of Agriculture. July 1971.

Farm Labor. Statistical Research Series. Washington, D.C.: U.S. Department of Agriculture, Crop Reporting Board. January 1967.

Fuller, Varden. "Factors Influencing Farm Labor Mobility." In *Labor Mobility and the Population in Agriculture.* Ames: Iowa State University, Center for Agricultural and Economic Adjustment. 1961.

Garnett, Bernard E. "Nonwhite Farmers Hit USDA Policies." *Race Relations Reporter* (Spring 1971).

Good Neighbor Commission. *Texas Migrant Labor.* Annual report. Austin, Texas. 1970.

Good, Paul. *Cycle to Nowhere.* Clearinghouse Publication No. 14. Washington, D.C.: U.S. Commission on Civil Rights. 1968.

Grubbs, Donald. *Cry from the Cotton.* Chapel Hill: The University of North Carolina Press. 1971.

Hathaway, Dale E. "Occupational Mobility from the Farm Labor Force." In *Farm Labor in the United States.* Edited by C. E. Bishop. New York: Columbia University Press. 1967.

—————; and Perkins, Brian B. "Farm Labor Mobility, Migration, and Income Distribution." *American Journal of Agricultural Economics* (May 1968).

—————; and Perkins, Brian B. "Occupational Mobility and Migration from Agriculture." In *Rural Poverty in the United States.* President's National Advisory Commission on Rural Poverty. Washington, D.C.: U.S. Government Printing Office. 1968.

Heady, Earl O.; and Kreng, Ronald D. *Farm Size and Cost Relationships in Relation to Recent Machine Technology.* Iowa Agricultural and Home Economics Experiment Station Bulletin No. 504. 1962.

Hennessy, J. L. "Employment of 'Green Card' Aliens during Labor Disputes." Presented during hearings of the Special Subcommittee on Labor of the House Committee on Education and Labor, 91st Cong., 1st Sess. Washington, D.C.: U.S. Government Printing Office. 1969.

Hightower, Jim. "Hard Tomatoes, Hard Times." *Society* (November-December 1972).

Ihnen, Loren; and Heady, Earl O. *Cost Functions in Relation to Farm Size and Machine Technology in Southern Iowa.* Iowa Agricultural and Home Economics Experiment Station Research Bulletin No. 527. 1964.

Johnson, D. Gale. "Comparability of Labor Capacities of Farm and Nonfarm Labor." *American Economic Review* (June 1953).

Johnson, Paul F. "Labor Mobility: Some Costs and Returns." In *Rural Poverty in the United States.* President's National Advisory Commission on Rural Poverty. Washington, D.C.: U.S. Government Printing Office. 1968.

Levitan, Sar A. *The Great Society's Poor Law*. Baltimore: The Johns Hopkins University Press. 1969.

Lovell, Malcolm. "Statement" before the Subcommittee on Agriculture and Labor of the House Committee on Education and Labor, June 30, 1971.

Madden, J. Patrick. *Economies of Size in Farming*. Washington, D.C.: U.S. Department of Agriculture, Economic Research Service. February 1967.

——————; and Partenheimer, Earl J. "Evidence of Economies and Diseconomies of Farm Size." In *The Size, Structure, and Future of Farms*. Edited by A. Gordon Ball and Earl O. Heady. Ames: Iowa State University Press. 1972.

Maddox, James. "An Historical Review of the Nation's Efforts to Cope with Rural Poverty." *Journal of Farm Economics* (December 1968).

Manpower Report to the President. Washington, D.C.: U.S. Government Printing Office. 1971.

Marshall, Patricia. "From Migrant Stream to Mainstream." *Manpower* (July 1971).

Masters, Stanley H. *A Study of Socioeconomic Mobility among Urban Negroes*. Final report to the Office of Economic Opportunity. New Brunswick, New Jersey: Rutgers University. 1970.

McCoy, John L. *Rural Poverty in Three Southern Regions: Mississippi Delta, Ozarks, Southeast Coastal Plains*. Agricultural Economics Report No. 176. Washington, D.C.: U.S. Department of Agriculture, Economic Research Service. March 1970.

McDonald, Stephen L. "Economic Factors in Farm Outmigration: A Survey and Evaluation of the Literature." Paper prepared for *Human Resource Development in the Rural South*. Austin: University of Texas, Center for the Study of Human Resources. 1971. Final report to the Office of Economic Opportunity. Mimeographed.

McElroy, Robert S. "Migratory Farm Worker Problems." Remarks to the National Manpower Advisory Committee, June 18, 1971.

McKee, Vernon C.; and Day, Lee M. "Measuring the Effects of Agricultural Programs on Income Distribution." In *Rural Poverty in the United States*. President's National Advisory Commission on Rural Poverty. Washington, D.C.: U.S. Government Printing Office. 1968.

Moyer, D. O.; *et al. Land Tenure in the United States: Development and Status.* Agricultural Information Bulletin No. 338. Washington, D.C.: U.S. Department of Agriculture, Economic Research Service. June 1969.

Myrdal, Gunnar. *An American Dilemma.* New York: Harper & Brothers. 1944.

New York *Times,* March 22, 1971; August 3, 1971; and October 4, 1971.

Nikolitch, R. "Family-Size Farms in U.S. Agriculture." ERS No. 499. Washington, D.C.: U.S. Department of Agriculture, Economic Research Service. February 1972.

Office of Equal Opportunity. *1971 Annual Report.* Washington, D.C.: U.S. Department of Agriculture. July 1972.

—————. *1971 Annual Report.* Washington, D.C.: U.S. Department of Labor. 1971.

Perkins, Brian B.; and Hathaway, Dale E. *The Movement of Labor between Farm and Nonfarm Jobs.* Agricultural Experiment Station Research Bulletin No. 13. East Lansing: Michigan State University. 1966.

Proceedings of the Workshop on Methods of Working with Limited Resource Farmers. U.S. Department of Agriculture, Tennessee Valley Authority, and fifteen southern universities. Washington, D.C.: U.S. Department of Agriculture. 1972.

Rodefeld, Richard O. "A Reassessment of the Status and Trends in 'Family' and 'Corporate' Farms in U.S. Society." Paper delivered at the First National Conference on Land Reform, San Francisco, April 25–28, 1973.

Santos, Richard. "Migrants and Social Services in Michigan: A Report on the 1970 Migrant Situation." February 25, 1971.

Sjaastad, Larry A. "The Costs and Returns to Human Migration." In *Labor Mobility and the Population in Agriculture.* Ames: Iowa State University, Center for Agricultural and Economic Adjustment. 1961.

Smith, Eldon D. "Nonfarm Employment Information for Rural People." *Journal of Farm Economics* (August 1966).

Study Committee on Cooperative Extension. *A People and a Spirit.* U.S. Department of Agriculture and National Association of State

Universities and Land Grant Colleges. Washington, D.C.: U.S. Department of Agriculture. 1968.

Sullivan, Ronald. "Puerto Ricans Check Jersey Farm Camps." New York *Times*. September 13, 1971.

Sundquist, W. B. "Economics of Scale and Some Impacts of Agricultural Policy on Farm Size." Paper prepared for *Human Resource Development in the Rural South*. Austin: University of Texas, Center for the Study of Human Resources. 1971. Final report to the Office of Economic Opportunity. Mimeographed.

U.S. Department of Agriculture. *Census of Agriculture*. Washington, D.C.: U.S. Government Printing Office. 1972.

U.S. Government Organizational Manual, 1971–1972. Washington, D.C.: U.S. Government Printing Office. 1972.

Van Arsdall, Roy M.; and Elder, William A. *Economies of Size of Illinois Cash-Grain and Hog Farms*. Urbana: University of Illinois Agricultural Experiment Station Bulletin No. 733. February 1969.

Washington *Post*. "U.S. Policy Handcuffs Small Farmers." October 5, 1971.

Wertheimer, Richard F., II. *The Monetary Rewards of Migration within the United States*. Washington, D.C.: Urban Institute. 1970.

3. Rural Nonfarm Employment

ONE OF THE most important requirements for improving the conditions of rural people is jobs. However, economic development specialists disagree about the feasibility or desirability of industrializing rural areas because of the limited attractions these areas are supposed to have for employers. In this view, measures to relocate rural people from labor surplus areas to growth centers would be more economical. This chapter examines this issue. The feasibility of relocation projects to move people out of rural areas is analyzed in chapter 4.

RURAL INDUSTRIALIZATION

An analysis of rural industrialization requires some attention to the effects of "natural" developments as well as to programs to divert industry from these "natural" sites. Unfortunately, however, industry is already so heavily subsidized that we do not know whether rural industrialization has been "natural" or induced. For whatever reason, though, rural areas in the United States have experienced surprisingly high rates of growth in nonfarm employment, especially in manufacturing. A study of twelve southeastern states for 1940 through 1960 found that urban (i.e., standard metropolitan statistical area, SMSA) counties gained more nonprimary (i.e., excepting agricultural and extractive) employment than nonurban counties relatively, but that urban and nonurban areas were almost equal in absolute terms. However, the nonurban counties gained more manufacturing employment absolutely and relatively. Indeed the urban share of manufacturing employment declined from 40.9 to 39.5 percent during this period (Goodstein, 1970, p. 397).

Although comparable data are not available for the 1960s, a USDA study shows manufacturing employment to have grown faster absolutely and relatively between 1962 and 1969 in small southern labor market areas (which include smaller SMSAs as well as rural areas). This study found 60 percent of the annual increase in manufacturing jobs to have been outside the 193 large metropolitan labor markets in the South. Moreover, the South was the only region where manufacturing job gains were larger absolutely in nonmetropolitan than in metropolitan areas during these years; 84,000 jobs were added in large metropolitan areas, a gain of 4.4 percent, while nonmetropolitan areas added 99,000 manufacturing jobs, a 5.3 percent gain (Haren, 1970, pp. 431–37).

There is some question about the nature of rural industrialization because of the imprecise definition of the areas covered. "Rural" and "nonmetropolitan" could mean the growth of industry on the fringes of major metropolitan areas, or they could cover industrialization which was some distance from major SMSAs.

The first reaction to the finding that manufacturing employment had grown faster during the 1960s in nonmetropolitan areas than in metropolitan areas was that this must be a metropolitan fringe phenomenon — i.e., the rural growth areas really were on the outskirts of large urban areas and therefore related to those areas, or it was insignificant in an absolute, if not relative, sense. In order to test this hypothesis, Till (1972) collected data for counties fifty miles from SMSAs in thirteen southern states. When this was done, it was found that nonfarm employment increased by 48.9 percent in the distant nonmetropolitan counties between 1959 and 1969, or an absolute increase of 674,345 jobs; the increase in nonfarm employment in the SMSAs was 49.7 percent, or an absolute increase in jobs of 2,811,677.

In manufacturing employment, the distant rural counties grew by 61.1 percent and the SMSAs by 47.7 percent; the absolute increases in manufacturing employment were 308,972 and 701,916 jobs, respectively. Growth in the SMSA fringe counties (within a fifty-mile radius of an SMSA) was relatively less in both nonfarm (48.3 percent) and manufacturing employment than in the more distant nonmetropolitan labor markets. Thus the composite picture does not support the hypothesis that nonmetropolitan growth is an urban fringe phenomenon. Moreover, the amount of growth was not proportional to the size of the leading city in nonmetropolitan areas.

With respect to industry composition, the distant nonmetropolitan labor markets were not typical of national patterns. In the rest of the United States, the service sectors are growing faster than goods-producing sectors, but in the nonmetropolitan labor markets of the South, the opposite is true (57 and 52 percent, respectively). Moreover, even though it was a slow-growth industry nationally, manufacturing was the "dynamic, fast-growth export sector" of nonmetropolitan labor markets. Almost half of the net increase in rural nonfarm jobs was in manufacturing. Indeed in 1970, manufacturing outnumbered farm jobs in the nonmetropolitan areas for the first time in the three states for which data were available (Arkansas, Mississippi, and South Carolina). This is probably typical for the entire South.

The kinds of industry most likely to locate in rural areas are different from those locating in urban areas, as indicated in Table 3-1. Industry locating in the rural South also is different from that in rural areas elsewhere. As compared with the United States as a whole, the South (as defined by the census) has relatively more of its labor force in the basic-resource-oriented industries of agriculture, forestry and fisheries, and mining and in personal services and construction. The United States has slightly more in finance, insurance, and real estate and in business and repair services and significantly more in durable goods manufacturing.

Urban areas have a higher percentage of workers in transportation, communications, and public utilities; wholesale and retail trade; finance, insurance, and real estate; all four service industries; and public administration.

While agriculture continued its secular decline between 1960 and 1970, urban areas actually increased their employment in this sector (see Table 3-2). This reflects the urbanization of many small towns where farmers reside and perhaps also the movement of some farmers to these small urban places. Mining follows the same pattern.

Personal services employment was declining everywhere, with the South experiencing the sharpest declines. Professional and related services was the fastest growth sector of all. However, this category grew about half as fast in the South as in the entire United States. Professional services grew slightly faster in urban than in rural areas in the United States and in the South.

The trends depicted in Tables 3-1 and 3-2 indicate a growing differentiation of economic activity in rural as contrasted with urban areas and between the South and the rest of the country. One of the most striking trends is the decline in agriculture, mining, and personal services

TABLE 3-1

Changes in Rural and Urban Employment, by Industry and Region
(1960–70)

Industry	South				United States			
	1960	1970	Absolute Change 1960–70	Percent Change 1960–70	1960	1970	Absolute Change 1960–70	Percent Change 1960–70
Urban:								
Agriculture, forestry and fisheries	182,919	204,716	21,797	11.92%	527,770	591,863	64,093	12.14%
Mining	145,569	165,253	19,684	13.52	297,635	324,425	26,790	9.00
Construction	781,885	997,731	215,846	27.61	2,612,891	3,107,516	494,625	18.93
Durable goods	986,010	1,477,088	491,078	49.80	7,540,984	8,824,885	1,283,901	17.03
Nondurable goods	1,391,296	1,593,506	202,210	14.35	5,407,167	5,799,871	-7,296	-0.13
Transportation, communications, and public utilities	900,803	1,108,375	207,572	23.04	3,546,903	4,109,966	563,063	15.87
Wholesale and retail trade	2,476,216	3,323,574	847,358	34.22	9,287,573	9,895,869	608,296	6.55
Finance, insurance, and real estate	551,496	828,198	276,702	50.17	2,344,174	3,318,709	974,535	41.57
Business and repair services	299,028	500,024	200,996	67.22	1,290,889	1,990,687	699,798	54.21
Personal services	1,100,640	993,961	-106,679	-9.69	2,995,013	2,757,637	-237,376	-7.93
Entertainment and recreation	98,394	130,757	32,363	32.89	422,157	532,736	110,579	26.19
Professional and related services	1,491,758	2,826,483	1,334,725	89.47	6,000,079	15,378,668	9,378,589	156.31
Public administration	811,537	1,125,940	314,403	38.74	2,588,884	3,420,479	831,595	32.12
Industries not reported	513,338				2,128,271			

Industry	South				United States			
	1960	1970	Absolute Change 1960–70	Percent Change 1960–70	1960	1970	Absolute Change 1960–70	Percent Change 1960–70
Rural:								
Agriculture, forestry and fisheries	1,603,030	813,355	–789,675	–49.26	3,822,114	2,248,625	–1,573,489	–41.17
Mining	193,665	164,505	–29,160	–15.06	356,371	306,363	–50,008	–14.03
Construction	518,288	667,251	148,963	28.74	1,203,046	1,464,719	261,673	21.75
Durable goods	658,338	922,894	264,556	40.19	2,287,705	2,916,132	628,427	27.47
Nondurable goods	943,339	1,263,941	320,602	33.99	1,877,230	2,296,320	419,090	22.32
Transportation, communications, and public utilities	335,005	433,826	98,821	29.50	911,244	1,076,135	164,891	18.10
Wholesale and retail trade	972,825	1,213,149	240,324	24.70	2,505,062	3,141,011	635,949	25.39
Finance, insurance, and real estate	117,604	186,881	69,277	58.91	350,456	519,678	169,222	48.29
Business and repair services	119,252	156,484	37,232	31.22	319,839	404,200	84,361	26.38
Personal services	432,794	376,929	–55,865	–12.91	863,481	778,939	–84,542	–9.79
Entertainment and recreation	27,050	34,230	7,180	26.54	80,722	98,457	17,735	21.97
Professional and related services	542,872	943,339	400,467	73.77	1,577,767	3,947,052	2,369,285	150.17
Public administration	245,570	327,117	81,547	33.21	614,006	781,173	167,167	27.23
Industries not reported	175,014				479,814			

SOURCE: Bureau of the Census, U.S. Department of Commerce, *Census of Population: 1960, United States Summary*, Table 91, and *Census of Population: 1970, General Social and Economic Characteristics, United States Summary*, Table 103 (Washington, D.C.: U.S. Government Printing Office).

TABLE 3-2

Employment Distribution by Region and Industry*
(1960, 1970)

Industry	Urban				Rural			
	South		United States		South		United States	
	1960	1970	1960	1970	1960	1970	1960	1970
Agriculture, forestry, and fisheries	1.56%	1.34%	1.11%	1.02%	23.28%	10.81%	22.16%	12.04%
Mining	1.24	1.08	0.63	0.56	2.81	2.19	2.07	1.64
Construction	6.67	6.53	5.51	5.37	7.53	8.87	6.97	7.84
Durable goods manufacturing	8.41	9.67	15.91	15.25	9.56	12.27	13.26	15.61
Nondurable goods manufacturing	11.86	10.43	11.41	10.02	13.70	16.80	10.88	12.29
Transportation, communication, and public utilities	7.68	7.25	7.48	7.10	4.87	5.77	5.28	5.75
Wholesale and retail trade	21.11	21.76	19.60	21.13	14.13	16.13	14.52	16.82
Finance, insurance, and real estate	4.70	5.43	4.95	5.73	1.71	2.48	2.03	2.78
Business and repair services	2.55	3.27	2.72	3.44	1.73	2.08	1.85	2.16
Personal services	9.38	6.51	6.32	4.76	6.29	5.01	5.01	4.17
Entertainment and recreation	0.84	0.86	0.89	0.92	0.39	0.46	0.47	0.53
Professional and related services	12.72	18.52	12.66	26.57	7.89	12.54	9.15	21.12
Public administration	6.92	7.37	5.46	5.91	3.57	4.35	3.56	4.18
Industries not reported	4.38		4.49		2.54		2.78	

* Percentage per industry.

SOURCE: Bureau of the Census, U.S. Department of Commerce, *Census of Population: 1970, General Social and Economic Characteristics, United States Summary*, Table 103, p. 509; *Census of Population: 1960, United States Summary*, Table 91 (Washington, D.C.: U.S. Government Printing Office).

and the growth of manufacturing in rural areas. However, in nonmetro-politan areas, the "professional and related services" category has been the fastest growing sector absolutely and relatively in the United States and the South, although the rate of change in this category was only about half as large in the South as in the rest of the United States. More-over, in the South the rural manufacturing sector as a whole (durable and nondurable) grew more absolutely between 1960 and 1970 than the professional and related services category; this was not true of the United States as a whole.

The rural South's employment is heavily concentrated in the rela-tively low-paying, nondurable manufacturing sector. Outside the South, the durable goods manufacturing sector is larger than the nondurable sector in urban and rural areas. In the South, the durable goods sector is growing much faster in urban areas (49.8 vs 14.53 percent), but the nondurable sector is growing faster in rural areas absolutely but not relatively. Significantly, the nondurable sector is declining in the urban United States and growing slightly in the urban South. Thus non-durable goods manufacturing is becoming a relatively rural industry in the United States and especially in the South.

Impact of Rural Industrialization

There is some question about the extent to which rural industrializa-tion provides jobs for the indigenous rural poor. The results of a study in Georgia and North Carolina indicate that industrialization of rural areas which provides even low-wage nonfarm employment to farm fami-lies can provide significant improvement in incomes for farm families (Hathaway, 1963, pp. 373–74). Low-wage industrialization also ap-pears to be a useful way to integrate industrial development with part-time farming. In many areas, farm women have been able to take non-farm jobs because mechanization of household and farm work has re-duced the time required for domestic work. Indeed in some areas of the rural South, there is concern about the implications of growing employ-ment for women and declining employment for men.

However, there is considerable evidence that industrialization often does not provide many job opportunities for poor people in rural areas. The extent to which jobs are provided seems to be a function of the nature of the industry and skill requirements. Although development economists usually urge the attraction of high-wage firms, these enter-prises often have the fewest employment effects for local people who are underemployed or unemployed. High-wage employers might not be able to find the skills they need in local labor markets, in which case skilled workers are imported from outside the area. In other cases, these firms find sufficient manpower among younger, better educated workers and therefore do not find it necessary to hire workers with limited education, even when the latter have the ability to do the work.

A number of studies have confirmed the limited impact of industrialization on local labor surpluses. In a study of the impact of a Kaiser Aluminum plant in West Virginia, Gray (1969) found that of four thousand jobs created only six hundred went to local people — the rest went to skilled outsiders. Similarly, a study in the Ozarks found industrialization to have bypassed the rural poor (Bender *et al.*, 1971). Another study of rural industrialization in the South found that the disadvantaged, particularly blacks, did not share proportionately in employment growth because new firms tended to "skim" local labor markets (Abt Associates, Inc., 1968; Wadsworth and Conrad, 1965, pp. 1197–1202).

The best data we have on the impact of industrialization on the rural poor are from a 1970 study conducted by the Economic Research Service of four nonmetropolitan growth areas, despite the fact that only 27 of 56 plants contacted agreed to cooperate (Kuehn *et al.*, 1970). This survey was of plants entering the areas after 1964 or significantly expanding after 1965. The areas chosen were in northeast Arizona, Mississippi, Appalachia, the Arkansas Ozarks, and the Arkansas delta. The study attempted to measure only the direct impact of industrialization on jobs, not indirectly created or induced jobs.

From the total sample of 991 jobs, 26.8 percent previously were poor, but there was considerable variation; 49 percent previously were poor in Arizona, as compared with 19 percent in Mississippi and the Arkansas Ozarks. The number of employees previously poor seems to depend on the amount of underemployment and manufacturing employment in the areas where the plants are located. However, the jobs in these plants were low paying and only raised 57 percent of the employees above the poverty level. Nearly a fourth (23.3 percent) of the poor workers hired in these plants were nonresidents.

With respect to the impact of rural industry by race, a study of nonmetropolitan areas of Mississippi found that industry seemed to avoid rural places with heavy concentrations of blacks and that blacks overshared in employment declines and undershared in growth (Till, 1972). Using changes in the proportion of persons below the poverty line in rapid- and slow-growth counties, this study found the rate of decline in poverty in slow-growth counties to be significantly less than in counties where manufacturing employment was growing rapidly. The same conclusion holds for blacks; their incidence of poverty declined more in the fast-growth counties, although blacks did not reduce their proportions in poverty as much as whites.

There is considerable additional evidence that blacks have not shared proportionately in the growth of nonmetropolitan industry in the South. For one thing, industry is growing mainly in predominantly white counties. Hansen found that the main factor common to those counties which grew during the 1960s after having declined in the 1950s was that they were predominantly white — even though they were in the nonmetropolitan South, the percentage of blacks in their population was less than that of the United States (Hansen, 1973).

Moreover, blacks do not share proportionately even in those manufacturing industries coming into predominantly black counties. To examine this question, Walker studied the impact of nonmetropolitan industry in 244 deep South counties with at least five thousand blacks in their population (Walker, 1974). Inadequate job opportunities largely account for the continued high rates of black migration from these counties, where white outmigration has declined to a very low level. These migration patterns tended to perpetuate the employment disadvantages of blacks because the younger, better educated blacks tend to migrate, leaving a residual population less competitive with whites who remain in those counties. However, other factors also accounted for the low occupational position of blacks in these counties, including the looseness of labor markets, occupation-skill requirements, and the ratio of manufacturing to total employment. Blacks have more difficulty getting rural jobs when unemployment is high and when industry skill requirements are high.

Disaggregating manufacturing, black areas are getting a proportionate share of employment in the lower paying, nondurable goods employment but not in the higher paying, durable goods sector. The main cause of the nature and quality of economic growth in the 244 deep South counties with large black populations was the limited education and work experience of the people in these counties who have depended heavily on plantation agriculture in the past. Growth industries tended to locate mainly in nonagricultural areas where people had some manufacturing or other nonfarm work experience. Moreover, the skill-occupational level of the work force was more important in the location of higher paying industry than education, although the latter was statistically significant.

Within the 244 deep South counties, blacks gained jobs, but at much less than their proportion of the population, and most of the job gains were at the lower paying levels. Blacks rarely got higher paying white-collar jobs. Of the variables explaining black job gains in the deep South, the expansion of employment was most important. However, the gains were weakened by black labor supply characteristics and labor market discrimination. Manufacturing was found to provide better opportunities for blacks in these counties than mining, wholesale and retail trade, finance, business repair, and public administration.

Black poverty in the 244 deep South counties declined during the 1960s in comparison to whites, but between a third and two-thirds of the improvement was due to outmigration. Economic growth accounted for between 9 and 22 percent of the decline in black poverty in these counties; by contrast, 26 percent of the decline in white poverty in these counties was attributable to economic development. Moreover, blacks actually gained a smaller percentage of the new jobs between 1960 and 1970 than they had between 1950 and 1960.

Rural-Urban Income Differentials

The conclusion that migration did little to reduce rural-urban income differentials (cited in chapter 2) is based largely on studies made before evidence from the 1970 census was available; the later information suggests very strongly that outmigration and rural industrialization are combining to reduce rural-urban income differentials. Data from the 1970 census indicate that rural areas have been gaining in comparison to urban areas since 1960, after having lost relatively between 1950 and 1960. As Table 3-3 shows, median farm income in the United States was 57.3 percent of the total in 1950 and 58.4 percent in 1960, but jumped to 78.8 percent in 1970. Rural nonfarm income was higher relatively, but declined from 80.9 percent of the national median in 1950 to 79.7 percent in 1960, but increased to 87.2 percent in 1970. At the same time, median urban incomes have declined relative to the national median: from 112.7 percent in 1950 to 105.7 percent in 1970.

The same patterns hold for the regions, except that before 1950 the farm-national median levels vary considerably from a low in the South to a high in the West. After 1950, the Northeast had the highest relative farm incomes. It also will be observed that urban incomes increased much less in comparison to the national median in the South (90.2 per-

TABLE 3-3

Median Income of Persons over Fourteen Years of Age, by Region (Selected years)

Category	United States Urban	United States Rural Nonfarm	United States Rural Farm	United States Total	South Urban	South Rural Nonfarm	South Rural Farm	South Total
Median income:								
1950	$2,162	$1,553	$1,099	$1,919	$1,740	$1,254	$ 787	$1,367
1960	3,136	2,250	1,649	2,823	2,542	1,746	1,171	2,120
1970	4,340	3,500	3,236	4,108	3,814	3,130	2,700	3,546
Median as a percentage of regional total median (1950)	112.7%	80.9%	57.3%		127.3%	91.7%	57.6%	
Median as a percentage of national median, by type (urban median, region/urban median, nation)					80.5	80.8	71.6	
Median as a percentage of national median					90.7	65.4	41.0	71.2%
Median as a percentage of regional total median (1960)	111.1	79.7	58.4		119.9	82.4	55.2	
Median as a percentage of national median, by type (urban median, region/urban median, nation)					81.1	77.6	71.0	
Median as a percentage of national median					90.1	61.9	41.5	75.1
Median as a percentage of regional total median (1970)	105.7	87.2	78.8		107.6	88.3	76.1	
Median as a percentage of national median, by type (urban median, region/urban median, nation)					87.9	87.4	83.4	
Median as a percentage of national median					92.8	76.2	65.7	86.3

SOURCE: Bureau of the Census, U.S. Department of Commerce, *Census of Population, 1950, 1960, 1970, Detailed Characteristics, Final Report, U.S. Summary* (Washington, D.C.: U.S. Government Printing Office, 1953, 1964, 1973).

cent in 1950 to 92.8 percent in 1970) than was true of rural nonfarm incomes (65.4 to 76.2 percent) or farm incomes (41 to 65.7 percent). However, the South was the only region where median urban incomes gained relative to the national total median between 1950 and 1970.

Table 3-4 shows that median farm income has gained relative to rural nonfarm income in every region. Nevertheless, in 1970, urban median personal income was $4,340 as compared with $3,580 and $3,236 for the rural nonfarm and farm categories, respectively.

A similar pattern emerges if we compare per employee personal income in agricultural with nonagricultural sectors (Table 3-5). There was a relative deterioration in the agricultural-nonagricultural ratio between 1952 and 1956 and irregular improvements thereafter. The agricultural-nonagricultural per employee income ratio regained its 1950 level (0.710) in 1966 and remained relatively high thereafter. These statistics suggest that the rural poverty problem is less a matter of lack of improvement in rural incomes compared to those of urban areas than it is of the level and distribution of rural income.

SUBEMPLOYMENT

As noted in chapter 2, the ratio of available workers to full-time jobs in southern agriculture rose between 1950 and 1969. We do not have adequate measures of the relative degree of underemployment in rural or urban areas. Unemployment data are available, but this is an unsatisfactory measure of the looseness or tightness of a labor market because it does not measure part-time employment, those who are no longer looking for work because they have become discouraged, and

TABLE 3-4

Rural Farm Median Income as a Percentage of
Rural Nonfarm Median Income, by Region
(Selected years)

Year	United States	South	North Central	Northeast	West
1950	70.8%	62.8%	90.2%	78.1%	88.3%
1960	73.3	67.1	77.8	72.9	90.1
1970	90.4	86.3	95.4	84.1	94.8

SOURCE: Bureau of the Census, U.S. Department of Commerce, *Census of Populations, 1950, 1960, 1970, Detailed Characteristics, Final Report, U.S. Summary* (Washington, D.C.: U.S. Government Printing Office, 1953, 1964, 1973).

TABLE 3-5

Comparison of Employee Personal Income, Agricultural
and Nonagricultural Sources
(1950–71)

Year	Per Worker Income		Ratio of Agriculture to Nonagriculture
	Agriculture	Nonagriculture	
1950	$2,844	$ 4,004	0.710
1951	3,375	4,375	0.771
1952	3,396	4,659	0.729
1953	3,161	4,887	0.647
1954	2,972	5,040	0.590
1955	2,726	5,264	0.518
1956	2,834	5,480	0.517
1957	2,969	5,737	0.518
1958	3,487	5,948	0.586
1959	3,500	6,187	0.566
1960	3,422	6,338	0.540
1961	3,796	6,558	0.579
1962	4,136	6,835	0.605
1963	4,399	7,053	0.624
1964	4,563	7,361	0.620
1965	5,410	7,723	0.701
1966	6,252	8,160	0.766
1967	6,251	8,582	0.728
1968	6,581	9,206	0.715
1969	7,641	9,728	0.785
1970	8,144	10,351	0.787
1971	8,707	10,985	0.793

SOURCE: Calculated from *1971 Business Statistics*, U.S. Department of Commerce, Office of Business Economics, pp. 7 and 67; and "Farm Income Situation," Economic Research Service, U.S. Department of Agriculture (July 1972), p. 48.

employed heads of families who receive insufficient incomes to bring them above the poverty level. Since these other problems, particularly labor force participation, are likely to be more severe in rural areas, the unemployment rate will understate the looseness of rural labor markets relative to those of urban areas, especially for males.

We do not have figures for rural and urban areas, but rough calculations of a subemployment index for metropolitan and nonmetropolitan areas are presented in Table 3-6. Although the unemployment rates were roughly the same in metropolitan and nonmetropolitan areas, the nonmetropolitan subemployment rate was much higher for males; the male metropolitan subemployment index was 4.6 times the unemployment rate, but the same ratio for nonmetropolitan males was 6.1.

ECONOMIC VIABILITY OF RURAL AREAS

Some specialists question the value of industrialization strategies, not only because of their limited impact on the rural poor but also because of skepticism about the ability to implement such a strategy. Hansen (1971), for example, concludes on the basis of evidence from the United States and abroad that efforts to "force-feed" the economic development of large lagging regions are not only inefficient but also largely ineffective. Similarly, McDonald (1971) is skeptical of industrialization strategies because "artificially locating industry would involve an indefinite subsidy (and social cost reflecting nonoptimal loca-

TABLE 3-6

Estimated Subemployment, by Sex, for Metropolitan
and Nonmetropolitan United States
(1960, 1970)

Category	Population over Fourteen*	Civilian Labor Force	Participation Rate	Unemployment	Unemployment Rate
1960:					
Metropolitan					
Male	38,506,428	29,432,652	76.4%	1,438,918	4.9%
Female	41,584,183	15,171,316	36.5	788,726	5.2
Nonmetropolitan					
Male	22,808,866	16,330,017	71.6	856,800	5.2
Female	23,377,071	7,210,094	30.1	420,383	5.8
1970:					
Metropolitan					
Male	48,792,380	34,973,569	71.7	1,365,032	3.9
Female	53,810,392	22,023,279	40.9	1,106,448	5.0
Nonmetropolitan					
Male	22,689,524	15,150,219	66.8	618,832	4.1
Female	24,105,893	8,752,631	36.3	499,241	5.7

TABLE 3-6 (continued)

	Proportion of Employable Nonparticipants under 65**	Adjusted Employment Rate	Working Poor Family Heads†	Subemployment Rate
1960:				
Metropolitan				
Male	2,596,331	13.7%	NA	NA
Female	2,180,923	19.6	NA	NA
Nonmetropolitan				
Male	1,912,386	17.0	NA	NA
Female	1,312,976	24.0	NA	NA
1970:				
Metropolitan				
Male	4,356,663	14.8	1,274,835	17.8%
Female	2,539,928	14.8	397,912	16.5
Nonmetropolitan				
Male	2,353,482	17.0	1,398,807	25.0
Female	1,192,192	17.0	23,828	17.3

NA=not available.

* Changes to population over sixteen years of age in 1970.

** For males, the proportion used is 50 percent of nonparticipants; for females, the proportion is 10 percent. The calculated value is added both to the civilian labor force and the unemployment to calculate the adjusted employment rate.

† Working poor family heads are added to unemployment and adjusted unemployment to calculate the rate of subemployment.

SOURCE: Bureau of the Census, U.S. Department of Commerce, *Census of Population: 1960, Characteristics of Inhabitants* (Washington, D.C.: U.S. Government Printing Office, 1962); and Bureau of the Census, U.S. Department of Commerce, *Census of Population: 1970, General Social and Economic Characteristics* (Washington, D.C.: U.S. Government Printing Office, 1972).

tion), while subsidizing successful moves by farm people has a one-time, self-liquidating cost." Moreover, industrial development strategies often cause local governments to pay too much for industry through tax abatements which seriously reduce the ability of those governments to finance local services (Abt Associates, Inc., 1968; Haren, 1970).

These findings suggest a number of policy implications. First, there seems to be sufficient "natural" industrialization to cause considerable doubt about the necessity of industry subsidies. Second, if industry is subsidized as a means of reducing labor surpluses, employment decisions cannot be left entirely to private decision makers, who will naturally hire the most productive workers available in order to maximize profits. A program of subsidies might be geared to a stipulation that a certain proportion of work forces be hired from local residents certified by the employment service to be disadvantaged.

Third, public policy might encourage industrial development by cooperatives or community corporations whose motives are to provide employment for the disadvantaged, rather than to maximize profits. This does not mean, of course, that these organizations would operate at a loss, because there are *profitable* activities in rural areas that private enterprises might avoid because they were not *the most profitable* investments they could make.

Fourth, there is some evidence that low-wage, labor-intensive industries are more effective in providing jobs for people with limited education and skills than capital-intensive industries with high skill requirements. Since industry tends to adapt to the kinds of work forces available, local areas might attempt to upgrade the kinds of industry they attract by investment in education and skills, as some southern states are trying to do. However, many people are likely to work in marginal jobs even if they migrate voluntarily or are relocated, so it might be effective public policy to provide limited subsidies to marginal industry, especially if employment in those industries also has desirable social consequences. Any strategy to improve the incomes of poor people must give heavy weight to noneconomic causes and benefits. For example, it might be more desirable to subsidize self-help activities that would make people largely (say, 80 percent) self-sufficient than to provide straight transfer payments to people who could not benefit from relocation or other manpower efforts. In other words, industrialization has had limited impact on rural labor surpluses, but a marginal industrialization strategy could be good public policy if safeguards were adopted to ensure that the disadvantaged were employed in the firms brought in. Many firms would not require subsidies but would be attracted by such services as good information about local labor markets, effective training programs, and indications that local leaders had favorable attitudes toward industry. Nevertheless, these kinds of activities probably are more influential in determining the particular place within which a firm locates after it makes a decision to locate in a certain larger area than they are in attracting firms that might have gone to other regions.

Growth Centers

Another approach to rural areas is a growth center strategy designed "to promote the development of lagging regions by concentrating in-

vestment geographically so as to reap scale and agglomeration economies. In addition, growth centers also have been conceived as points
of attraction for migrants who otherwise would go to large, congested
areas" (Hansen, 1971). However, Hansen, a leading authority on
growth centers, concludes on the basis of studies in the United States
and abroad: "To date these strategies have not been notably successful,
primarily because they have suffered from a tendency toward prolifera-
tion of a large number of relatively small centers. Moreover, even where
a few large centers have been selected, inadequate funding has been a
problem."

There also is a serious conceptual problem with growth center
strategies because they are not based on theoretical underpinnings that
would, according to Hansen, provide "specific criteria for identifying the
location of relevant urban centers, how big they should be, or what kinds
of investments should be placed in them."

Lindley (1969) believes that cities of 25,000 to 500,000 have the
greatest growth potential for the 1970s and advocates building a

> . . . growth center strategy on that natural economic growth
> process. The growth center strategy is an attempt through public
> policy to reinforce the natural growth in population and employ-
> ment of many . . . urban communities . . . and to attempt to divert
> the future flow of rural or small town migrants to keep them
> away from the center city of the large cities.

Lindley concedes, however, that growth center strategy is in its in-
fancy in the United States, even though it is being pursued in Canada
and Europe. Moreover, the American experiences (Appalachian Regional Commission and Economic Development Administration) are,
in his words,

> . . . isolated economic development strategies and are not coupled
> with a complementary national urban growth and manpower
> development strategy. To put it another way, these are efforts to
> create employment opportunities with the necessary comple-
> mentary policies of supporting a rapid expansion in the physical
> development of the community such as housing for low-income
> families. . . . Effective efforts have yet to be made to relate a
> growth center . . . strategy with a complementary national re-
> settlement assistance policy and manpower training and develop-
> ment policy to assist in the transition from rural life to an urban
> employment environment.

The Rural Development Act of 1972

The passage of the Rural Development Act of 1972 gives some promise of promoting rural development that will benefit the disadvantaged as well as those who traditionally benefit from agricultural programs. Since the provisions of the Act are to be administered by the USDA, there also is some hope that responsibility for a broader range of rural activities will shift that department's interests away from its narrow agribusiness emphasis toward broader rural development concerns. Taken literally, the provisions of the Act could provide considerable employment directly in constructing community facilities and new businesses and indirectly in the ongoing employment in new or expanded industrial activities. The Act also provides for increased research on problems of small farmers. Since community corporations, cooperatives, and nonprofit organizations are eligible along with profit-making organizations and government agencies for loans and grants, the Act could stimulate some institutions to concern themselves with the problems of the rural disadvantaged.

The Act is a collection of many different legislative authorities. It provides for:

(1) Rural industrialization loans to public or private, profit or nonprofit organizations to promote business development and improve the environmental climate in rural areas, including pollution control.

(2) Insured or guaranteed small business loans to individuals. If private sources are not available for credit, the borrower may secure funds from the Farmers Home Administration or directly from the Secretary of Agriculture.

(3) A number of provisions designed to promote community development, including:

(a) Community facility grants to public agencies in towns with populations of ten thousand or less. These grants are to be used to facilitate economic development.

(b) Community facility loans, insured or guaranteed, at 5 percent interest.

(c) Grants and technical assistance for water and sewer facilities and community fire protection.

(d) Guarantee of housing loans for rural people whose incomes are too high for them to qualify for Farmers Home Administration low- to moderate-income loans.

(e) Three new research and education programs: rural development extension; rural development research; and small farm extension, research, and development. Research funds are to be administered by land grant universities in each state, but all colleges and universities are eligible to participate.

(f) Comprehensive planning grants to public agencies or "such other agencies as the Secretary may select."

Although the Act could be very significant for rural development by creating new jobs, providing many needed public facilities, and meeting some of the research needs of small farmers, some close observers of rural development and federal politics are not optimistic that the Act's potential will be realized. There are a number of causes for this pessimism:

(1) President Nixon signed the Act reluctantly, causing doubts about how enthusiastically he will support its major provisions. He favored measures to provide rural community development special revenue sharing, a department of community development, and new loan authority for commercial, industrial, and community development under a credit-sharing system which would permit states to select loan recipients. There is a question of whether or not the Nixon administration would impound funds for the Rural Development Act if they were appropriated by Congress.

(2) Another cause of uncertainty is the fact that responsibility for the Rural Development Act is lodged in the USDA which does not have a particularly good record for nonagricultural matters or for supporting low-income farmers. The USDA's traditional constituency has been a very small part of the rural population. Therefore it probably lacks both the expertise and the inclination to do the kinds of things needed to provide rural development for the benefit of all groups. On the other hand, many hope the new authority will strengthen those elements within the USDA more sympathetic to human resource development.

(3) Finally, even if funding, political, and administrative problems were solved, the Rural Development Act would be limited because it does not contain an adequate conceptual framework for a rural development policy. The Act merely contains a collection of 28 major authorities (and a number of minor

ones), many of which were already covered in previous legislation. It is hoped that if the Rural Development Act is adequately funded, it will stimulate the formulation of a conceptual framework for a rural development policy.

SUMMARY AND CONCLUSIONS

Although agricultural employment is declining in rural areas, nonfarm employment has grown relatively fast, particularly in the nondurable goods manufacturing sector. Moreover, at least in the South, rural manufacturing employment growth is not an urban fringe phenomenon, because growth has been faster in rural counties fifty miles from SMSAs than in the SMSAs themselves. The composition of rural nonfarm employment differs considerably from that of urban areas. Much rural industrialization is relatively low wage and requires very limited skills. This is particularly true in places where agriculture has predominated and provides the main economic background for nonfarm work forces. Marginal nonfarm jobs in these areas make it possible for farm families to supplement their income by providing jobs to wives and other family members. Higher wage industry apparently is attracted primarily to rural places where marginal manufacturing activities already provide nonfarm work experience and training.

The kinds of industry coming into rural areas have had different effects on various groups, depending mainly on the character of the industry and the nature of local labor supplies. Marginal industry provides more employment, but at wages so low as to have a limited impact on elevating people above the poverty level. Capital-intensive, higher wage industry provides fewer jobs but does more to elevate the incomes of those who get jobs.

Whites have benefited from rural industrialization more than blacks in the South, where almost all rural blacks are located. There is fairly consistent evidence that the fastest economic growth occurs outside areas with heavy black populations. Although blacks have shared in rural job gains in the heavily black counties of the South, they have not gained relative to their proportion of the population and therefore have been forced to continue their heavy migration out of the rural South, even though the white rate of outmigration declined considerably during the 1960s. Blacks were particularly underrepresented in higher paying white-collar jobs.

The immediate reasons for inadequate black participation are not clear. There is little doubt that discrimination and black concentration in plantation agriculture, which limited human resource development, are important ultimate causes of black economic disadvantage. As might be expected, in the deep South black counties, blacks got jobs mainly where manufacturing employment growth was greatest but also where education and industry skill requirements were relatively low. Education was a statistically significant factor explaining black occupational positions, but it was much less important than nonfarm work experience. Finally, the rate of poverty declined among blacks in the 244 counties with relatively large black populations, but apparently more because of outmigration than because of rising job opportunities.

This chapter also demonstrated that the rural-urban income gap is closing because rural incomes are rising relative to the national median while those of urban areas are declining. These income movements are caused mainly by rural-to-urban and farm-to-nonfarm population shifts, rising farm incomes as farm productivity increases, and rising nonfarm incomes as rural areas industrialize. Although farm incomes have increased faster, the nonfarm-urban income gap is smaller than the farm-urban income gap. All evidence points to a continued narrowing of these rural-urban income gaps.

Despite the improvements in relative incomes of rural areas, some rural economic problems remain, especially a heavy incidence of poverty, subemployment, and unequal income distribution.

In order to ameliorate these problems, rural economic development must be accelerated and the benefits of industrialization more widely and evenly dispersed. Although there is some doubt about the economic viability of rural areas, the evidence suggests that the proper rural development policies could help solve the problems of blacks and other disadvantaged rural people. An important component of an economic development strategy must be rural manpower programs, considered in chapter 4.

REFERENCES

Abt Associates, Inc. *The Industrialization of Southern Rural Areas: A Study of Industry and Federal Assistance in Small Towns with Recommendations for Future Policy.* Conducted for the Economic Development Administration, U.S. Department of Commerce. 1968.

Bender, Lloyd; *et al.* "Trickle Down and Leakage in the War on Poverty." *Growth and Change* (October 1971).

Goodstein, Marvin E. "A Note on Urban and Nonurban Employment Growth." *Journal of Regional Science* (December 1970).

Gray, Irwin. "New Industrialization in a Rural Area." *Monthly Labor Review* (June 1969).

Hansen, Niles M. "Growth Centers, Human Resources, and Rural Development." Paper prepared for *Human Resource Development in the Rural South*. 1971.

————. *The Future of Nonmetropolitan America*. Lexington, Massachusetts: D. C. Heath. 1973.

Haren, Claude C. "Rural Industrial Growth in the 1960's." *American Journal of Agricultural Economics* (August 1970).

Hathaway, Dale E. *Government and Agriculture*. New York: Macmillan Publishing Company. 1963.

Kuehn, John A.; *et al. Impact of Job Development on Poverty in Four Developing Areas*. Agricultural Economics Report No. 225. Economic Research Service, U.S. Department of Agriculture. 1970.

Lindley, Jonathan. "The Geographic Dimension of a Full Employment Policy." Paper presented to the National Manpower Advisory Committee, June 20, 1969.

McDonald, Stephen L. "Economic Factors in Farm Outmigration: A Survey and Evaluation of the Literature." Austin, Texas: Center for the Study of Human Resources. 1971.

Till, Thomas E. "Rural Industrialization and Southern Rural Poverty in the 1960's: Patterns of Labor Demand in Southern Nonmetropolitan Labor Markets and Their Impact on Rural Poverty." Austin: University of Texas, Center for the Study of Human Resources. 1972. Mimeographed.

Wadsworth, Henry A.; and Conrad, James M. "Leakages Reducing Employment and Income Multipliers in Labor Surplus Rural Areas." *Journal of Farm Economics* (December 1965).

Walker, James L. "Economic Development, Black Employment, and Black Migration in the Nonmetropolitan Deep South." Austin: University of Texas, Center for the Study of Human Resources. 1974. Mimeographed.

4. Rural Manpower Programs

THERE IS almost universal agreement among economic development specialists that manpower programs to match workers with present and future jobs are indispensable parts of any rural development strategy. Functionally, manpower programs provide:

(1) Training, whether on the job, in classrooms, or some combination of the two

(2) Preemployment supportive activities to help workers prepare for training or employment

(3) Public employment programs for people who cannot find private jobs or become self-employed without intolerable levels of inflation or at some distance from their homes

(4) Measures to improve the operation of the labor market through better information about job opportunities in various places and about workers available for these jobs, removing discrimination and other obstacles to the employment of otherwise qualified workers, and relocation assistance to move workers from labor surplus to labor shortage areas

Manpower programs alone cannot promote rural development, but when combined with other measures (especially education and health, housing, welfare, income maintenance, and industrial development activities) can do much to promote industrialization.

The essential economic problems of rural areas are to provide income or employment for the unemployed or underemployed, to upgrade work forces, and to facilitate the movement of people from labor surplus areas

89

to other areas where jobs are more plentiful. Manpower programs could play an important role in both the process of industrialization and the movement of people to where job opportunities exist. These programs also could facilitate industrialization by providing potential employers with information about local labor markets, helping employers train their work forces, and providing training for unemployed workers or upgrading training for those who are employed. Indeed the Labor Department has a number of programs designed to facilitate the use of manpower in economic development, and some states have made manpower an integral part of their industrial development activities because they realize that the kinds of firms attracted are strongly influenced by the quality of potential work forces. Higher income-paying firms are likely to be attracted by educated and trained work forces.

This chapter examines some of the efforts to extend manpower services to rural areas. It starts with an overview of rural manpower programs and then examines some major rural manpower programs and issues in greater depth.

OVERVIEW

Traditionally, the federal-state employment service, through the Farm Labor Service, has concentrated mainly on meeting the seasonal farm needs of employers and has done very little to help farm workers acquire nonagricultural jobs. In order to become more effective in rural areas, the Labor Department created the Rural Manpower Service in 1971. The immediate aim was to use existing staff more effectively in providing "equity of access" to manpower services for all groups in rural areas. However, even after the service was created, delivery of rural manpower services was limited by inadequate funds, by frequent isolation of the former farm labor specialist from the mainstream of rural manpower activities, and by inflexibility of the local employment office's organizational structure. The Rural Manpower Service is experimenting with the following three pilot projects to improve delivery:

(1) Operation Hitchhike is attempting to attach manpower programs to existing rural institutions in order to reach scattered rural populations more effectively. There were fourteen such projects in fiscal year 1974.

(2) The Ottumwa Plan (or Area Concept Expansion program), which seeks to link central manpower service centers with feeder units reaching into the hinterland but drawing on the expertise of the central office, gives considerable promise of meeting some

of the problems involved in delivering manpower services to thinly populated rural areas. There were nine such projects in fiscal year 1974.

(3) The National Migrant Worker Program (discussed in chapter 2) is designed to make it possible for migrants to leave the migrant stream.

In addition, the Labor Department has a number of ongoing rural manpower pilot projects. One of these is the Smaller Communities Program operating in nineteen states. Under this program, traveling teams of specialists carry manpower services into rural areas. Although training programs have not been too effective in rural areas, primarily because of inadequate training facilities, rural workers have participated in a number of regular manpower programs. In fiscal year 1970, for example, 250,000 people in rural counties were enrolled in work experience and training programs. Most of these enrollees were in Neighborhood Youth Corps programs (see Table 4-1), which could be a major vehicle for easing the rural-to-urban transition, since the majority of the rural youth will be migrating and in need of assistance. Under the Manpower Development and Training Act (MDTA), institutional and on-the-job training programs enrolled only about 35,700 rural people in 1972, and a very few of these were trained for expanding skilled farm jobs.

Rural workers participate in a number of other manpower programs. In 1970, about fourteen thousand trainees in 45 states participated in MDTA programs linked to economic development projects in chronic labor surplus areas. About 17,400 rural residents were enrolled in Operation Mainstream, designed to give meaningful work experience in public works to unemployed older workers. As of March 1974, Operation Mainstream programs operated in every state except Delaware. Because it concentrated on meaningful work and cooperated with community power structures, this program seems to have been fairly successful, although it provided very limited skills training and upgrading opportunities and did little to get its participants absorbed into private employment.

Another program designed specifically to help rural people is the Concerted Services in Training and Education project, which is defined as a pilot effort to improve smaller communities and rural areas by demonstrating that education and occupational training, in conjunction with other economic development activities, can significantly help in-

TABLE 4-1

Estimated Rural Enrollment in Selected Manpower Programs and
Funds Obligated for Rural Enrollees (Fiscal year 1972)

Program	New Enrollment	Estimated Rural Enrollment		Estimated Funds Obligated* (millions)	
		Number	Percent	Total	Rural Enrollees
MDTA institutional	150,600	29,200	19.4%	$ 355.7	$ 69.0
National contracts (on-the-job training)	24,800	6,500	26.2	19.3	5.1
Neighborhood Youth Corps:					
In school	186,000	28,850	15.5	74.9	11.6
Out of school	65,000	20,400	31.4	122.0	38.3
Summer	759,900	174,600	23.0	320.4	73.7
Operation Mainstream	31,400	17,400	55.4	85.4	47.2
Concentrated Employment Program	84,700	18,800	22.2	154.6	34.3
Job Opportunities in the Business Sector	82,800	10,350	12.5	118.2	14.8
Work Incentive Program	120,600	14,350	11.9	174.8	20.8
Public Service Careers	27,000	3,150	11.7	38.0	7.2
TOTAL**	1,532,800	323,600	21.1	$1,463.1	$322.0

* Estimate derived by applying the percentage of rural enrollment to total obligations.
** Total does not include several programs for which urban-rural data are not available.

SOURCE: Subcommittee of Rural Development of the Committee on Agriculture and Forestry, United States Senate, *Manpower Training and Employment Programs Serving Rural America* (Washington, D.C.: U.S. Government Printing Office, 1973), p. 10.

crease employment opportunities. This project was suggested by a Cabinet-level rural development committee and organized by a sixteen-member task force. It seeks to:

(1) Develop means for concentrating interagency resources on the problems of people in selected communities
(2) Identify employment opportunities and occupational education programs for the poor and unemployed
(3) Develop ways in which rural communities can promote human resource development
(4) Demonstrate the potential of human resource development programs to improve employment opportunities
(5) Demonstrate the value of local involvement in human resource development programs

In order to accomplish these objectives, seventeen Concerted Services in Training and Education pilot projects were established in thirteen states by the end of fiscal year 1971.

An evaluation of the Concerted Services in Training and Education project (McCauley, September-October 1971) shows that it had improved training opportunities, increased use of the public employment service, provided local leaders with valuable information and consulting services, and developed additional job opportunities. Moreover, according to this evaluation, "this project is long on ideas and dedication of personnel, low on cost, with benefits that appear to be highly promising" (McCauley, p. 9).*

There were also thirteen rural Concentrated Employment Programs in 1970. Although there is some controversy about the effectiveness of the rural programs in achieving their objective of concentrating a variety of manpower resources in order to improve the job opportunities of poor people in rural areas, a national evaluation of five rural Concentrated Employment Programs concluded that they had improved the employment and incomes of their participants (who not only obtained better and more stable jobs but also improved their levels of living markedly). The rural programs also demonstrated considerable flexibility in adjusting to the diverse training, economic development, and work experience realities in their areas. This adaptability was necessary because the basic Concentrated Employment Program concept was designed for concentrated urban populations and not for scattered target groups in a

---

* For the full evaluation, see Griessman, 1969.

number of political entities in rural areas. Not all observers agree that these programs have been worth their cost. In its paper "A Rural Manpower Strategy," for example, the Rural Manpower Service concludes:

> . . . [The] difficulty in adopting the concentrated aspect of the urban program model has been great. Rural CEPs are very expensive, and it is doubtful that the results justify the expense involved. The concept of the rural CEP should be closely examined to see if the expense could be diverted into a more effective delivery system.

Rural governments have also participated in the Public Service Careers and Emergency Employment Act programs which are designed to open government jobs to the unemployed and disadvantaged. Since many government programs operate in rural areas, public employment offers considerable promise as a means of providing employment. However, these programs have been limited because so few rural governments have merit systems (which are required for Public Service Careers participation) or personnel to administer the programs. Rural participation in Emergency Employment Act programs has been limited because the allocation formula (unemployment) used by this agency discriminates against rural areas and because its framers were not sufficiently sensitive to the unique problems of rural areas. Although rural areas have been disadvantaged by the Act, they have benefited from provisions which allocate funds to American Indians on reservations, migrant workers, and counties with a population of 75,000 or less (by March 1972, rural counties had received 29 percent of the funds provided under this section). Nevertheless, if restructured, public employment programs could do much to provide employment to the unemployed and underemployed in rural areas, many of whom are not likely to be absorbed by private enterprise unless economic expansion is much greater than it is likely to be. General economic measures could not reduce rural unemployment and subemployment without intense inflation.

Table 4-2 gives information on the characteristics of rural people enrolled in selected manpower programs. Except for the part-time institutional training program, the rural enrollees were overwhelmingly poor or otherwise disadvantaged. Except for the Work Incentive Program, Phase II of the Neighborhood Youth Corps, and the New Careers program, a majority of the enrollees were males.

TABLE 4-2

Key Characteristics of Rural Residents Enrolled in Selected
Manpower Programs (In percentages for fiscal year 1972)

Characteristic	Operation Mainstream	Work Incentive Program	Concentrated Employment Program	MDTA Institutional Regular	Part-time
Sex:					
Male	70.0%	47%	60%	64%	75%
Female	30.0	53	40	36	25
Age:					
Under nineteen	0.2	12	14	14	5
Nineteen to 21	2.0	17	27	25	6
22 to 44	54.0	65	52	53	57
45 to 54	16.0	5	5	6	21
55 and older	28.0	1	2	2	10
Race:					
White	70.0	83	55	73	80
Black	15.0	13	35	20	10
American Indian	12.0	3	10	5	9
Asian American	2.0	*	*	1	1
Spanish-surnamed	3.0	4	5	3	1
Other	1.0	1	*	1	1
Education:					
Less than eight years	26.0	15	11	6	9
Eight years	18.0	15	11	7	11
Nine to eleven years	28.0	37	35	29	21
Twelve years or more	26.0	33	43	58	59
Military status:					
Veterans (total)	28.0	16	19	32	18
Nonveterans	72.0	84	81	68	82
Disadvantaged:					
Yes	92.0	92	99	66	20
No	8.0	8	1	34	80
Poverty:					
Yes	97.0	96	99	67	21
No	3.0	4	1	33	79
Family head:					
Yes	81.0	81	62	57	74
No	19.0	19	38	43	26

* Less than ½ of 1 percent.

TABLE 4-2 (continued)

| Characteristic | On-the-Job Training | Neighborhood Youth Corps | | New Careers |
		Out of School	Phase II	
Sex:				
Male	79.0%	54%	48%	32%
Female	21.0	46	52	68
Age:				
Under nineteen	10.0	91	96	5
Nineteen to 21	21.0	6	2	12
22 to 44	55.0	1	1	74
45 to 54	10.0	1	0	3
55 and older	4.0	1	2	4
Race:				
White	78.0	64	63	50
Black	17.0	25	33	42
American Indian	4.0	10	2	4
Asian American	0.5	*	1	2
Spanish-surnamed	1.0	5	5	11
Other	0.5	*	2	2
Education:				
Less than eight years	7.0	14	10	5
Eight years	8.0	21	19	3
Nine to eleven years	28.0	64	70	19
Twelve years or more	57.0	1	1	72
Military status:				
Veterans (total)	35.0	1	1	24
Nonveterans	65.0	99	99	76
Disadvantaged:				
Yes	41.0	97	99	94
No	59.0	3	1	6
Poverty:				
Yes	41.0	98	99	95
No	59.0	2	1	5
Family head:				
Yes	67.0	12	13	60
No	33.0	88	87	40

* Less than 1/2 of 1 percent.

SOURCE: Subcommittee of Rural Development of the Committee on Agriculture and Forestry, United States Senate, *Manpower Training and Employment Programs Serving Rural America* (Washington, D.C.: U.S. Government Printing Office, 1973), pp. 11, 12.

The foregoing examples are illustrations only and by no means exhaust the list of the Labor Department's rural manpower programs. Others include:

(1) A cooperative support program to help support the economic development activities of low-income cooperatives in rural areas.

(2) A farm foreman training program to teach labor relations to people involved with the supervision of farm labor.

(3) The Farm Labor Contractor Registration program, provided for by the Farm Labor Contractor Registration Act of 1963 and designed to protect migrant workers and their families from exploitation by farm labor contractors.

(4) The Indian program, designed to assure the delivery of manpower services to rural Indians.

(5) The Puerto Rico program, to provide manpower services to rural workers in Puerto Rico.

(6) The woods program, designed to alleviate a widespread shortage of workers in the woods industries by providing education and training for potential applicants.

(7) The Work Incentive Program, designed to use manpower services in an effort to ensure that employable welfare recipients will be furnished incentives, work experience, and supportive services to obtain permanent employment.

(8) A statewide Job Bank program, a computerized project to facilitate the timely and widespread distribution of job information in both urban and rural areas.

Table 4-3 provides some information on the geographic location of these programs.

THE RURAL MANPOWER SERVICE

The change in the Farm Labor Service to the Rural Manpower Service did not end the criticism of that agency, since it continued with many of the same personnel and many of the same procedures and with no additional funding for expanding services. With little control over powerful employers and rural interests, it was difficult for the Rural Manpower Service to champion the cause of relatively powerless rural workers. The agency has taken steps to train employment service and Farm Labor Service people so that they will serve as manpower agents for rural workers, nonfarm employers, and community groups.

TABLE 4-3

Selected Manpower Programs in Rural Areas by Region and State*

(June 30, 1972)

Region/State	Operation Hitch-hike	Area Concept Expansion	National Migrant Worker Program	Smaller Communities Program	Concerted Services in Training and Education	Rural Concentrated Employment Program	Co-op Support	Farm Foreman Training	Woods Program	Statewide Job Bank
Region I:										
Connecticut										x
Maine		x		x	x	x				x
Massachusetts										
New Hampshire										x
Rhode Island										x
Vermont	x	x		x						
Region II:										
New Jersey		x								x
New York	x		x**	x						x
Region III:										
Delaware										x
Maryland					x					x

	1	2	3	4	5	6	7	8
Pennsylvania								
Virginia			x			x		x
West Virginia					x	x		x
Region IV:								
Alabama			x			x		
Florida			x				x	
Georgia			x		x			x
Kentucky			x	x	x			x
Mississippi	x		x	x		x		x
North Carolina		x	x	x			x**	x
South Carolina			x	x	x			
Tennessee			x	x		x		
Region V:								
Illinois					x			x
Indiana							x	
Michigan	x			x	x	x	x	x
Minnesota				x	x	x		
Ohio							x	
Wisconsin				x		x	x	x

* Includes states where programs are in a rural county, defined as one in which 50 percent or more of the population is rural, as reported by the census.

** Funds appropriated but program not operating.

TABLE 4-3 (continued)

Selected Manpower Programs in Rural Areas by Region and State
(June 30, 1972)

Region/State	Operation Hitch-hike	Area Concept Expansion	National Migrant Worker Program	Smaller Communities Program	Concerted Services in Training and Education	Rural Concentrated Employment Program	Co-op Support	Farm Foreman Training	Woods Program	Statewide Job Bank
Region VI:										
Arkansas				X	X	X	X			X
Louisiana							X			X
New Mexico	X		X	X	X	X				X
Oklahoma		X		X	X		X			X
Texas			X	X	X		X			
Region VII:										
Iowa	X			X						
Kansas										X
Missouri		X				X	X			X*
Nebraska	X				X					
Region VIII:										
Colorado			X							

Montana						x				
North Dakota							x			
South Dakota		x								
Utah			x							
Wyoming					x					
Region IX:										
Arizona			x**			x				x
California			x	x				x		
Hawaii									x	x
Nevada		x			x					
Region X:										
Alaska	x			x						
Idaho	x	x	x		x					x
Oregon	x	x		x						x
Washington	x	x								x
TOTAL number of states	16	12	14	17	14	14	14	1	1	21

* As of August 1972.

** Funds appropriated but program not operating.

SOURCE: Division of Rural Program Development, Rural Manpower Service, U.S. Department of Labor (Washington, D.C., August 22, 1972).

Valuable information on the operation of the Rural Manpower Service was provided by a special review of that organization ordered by Secretary of Labor Hodgson following a public complaint in 1971 by the Migrant Legal Action Program. In its report, the review committee confirmed that the Farm Labor Service had been dominated by employers and was primarily responsive to their interests, mainly because farm workers were too weak to protect their interests. According to the Manpower Administration (1972, pp. 7–8):

> Farm worker organizations or unions were rare, and where they existed, they had not, relatively speaking, commanded a strong position. Without the economic and political power which comes from organization and solidarity, farm workers' interests suffered accordingly.

As noted earlier, the grower bias of the Farm Labor Service, along with the declining labor needs of agribusiness, prompted the Labor Department to create the Rural Manpower Service and make it a more rural worker-oriented agency. However, on the basis of the special ten-month review completed in 1972, Secretary Hodgson (New York *Times*, April 23, 1972, p. 2) conceded that "it is clear to us that our corrective measures have not been strong enough and in some cases have not been fully carried out."

The findings which led him to this conclusion were: First, the Rural Manpower Service in the field was still performing the traditional role of the Farm Labor Service. "While a few offices have made some changes, the ambitious redirection envisioned has in practical effect been more cosmetic than real" (Manpower Administration, 1972, p. 9). Moreover, "what was evident was that when [the Rural Manpower Service] errs, it errs in favor of the employer to the detriment of the worker." Even when the agency

> ... performs perfectly according to its own procedures, it is still doing a "Farm Labor Service" job which on the whole has been judged not fully relevant to the current needs of its worker constituents, and which often works to the detriment of the long-term interests of the worker and the local community.

Second, the farm worker remained powerless to influence his own condition. The Manpower Administration in its 1972 report said that the farm worker "is at a distinct disadvantage relative to all other workers because of his exclusion from or reduced coverage under social legislation, the inadequate enforcement of those laws which do protect him, and his lack of organization in dealing with farm employers" (pp. 10–11). The review team documented many cases where laws were ignored or violated because farm workers had no advocates to police the system, inform workers of their rights, and file complaints with enforcement agencies (p. 11).

Third, there were many cases where the Rural Manpower Service field offices conformed with patterns of race and sex discrimination in referrals. And fourth, it was demonstrated that the service field offices knowingly helped employers discriminate against domestic workers in favor of aliens. Before aliens are admitted to the United States, the Secretary of Labor or his agent must certify that domestic workers are not available and that the employment of foreigners will not adversely affect wages and working conditions of domestic workers. However, according to the review committee, the employment service makes *pro forma* efforts to recruit domestics in order to cater to the employer's desire to certify that none are available so that he can import foreigners.

The committee documented the depressing effects of foreign workers on domestic working conditions and concluded that employers preferred foreign workers because they would work for less money and would accept extremely poor working conditions. Foreign workers can be "kept in line" by threats of repatriation, and even poor wages and working conditions in the United States are often so superior to alternatives in their homeland that they are willing to work much harder than American citizens in order to keep their jobs. Foreign workers endure these conditions for relatively short periods of time in order to accumulate funds that will have higher purchasing power in their countries. In support of this, the Manpower Administration (1972, p. 37) tells us:

> A self-reinforcing cycle is thus created: foreign workers tend to depress wages; depressed wages discourage domestic workers from taking the jobs; and the inability to recruit domestic workers is used to justify the use of foreign workers. The result is the continuation and expansion of the use of foreign workers despite an oversupply of domestic workers.

Fifth, the Rural Manpower Service had done little to correct well-documented violations of even the inadequate labor laws covering agricultural workers: Social Security payments were deducted and not credited to workers' accounts, minimum wage and child labor laws were not enforced, little was done to halt the legal and illegal entry of foreign labor competition (there were documented cases where immigration officials refused to cooperate in the apprehension of illegal aliens), the

Farm Labor Contractor Registration Act of 1963 administered by the Rural Manpower Service was ignored by about half of all crew leaders (there is little or no incentive to register, and the crew leader avoids liability insurance and the cost of transportation safety requirements if he does not register), and the only thing the Rural Manpower Service will do if unregistered crew leaders are found is to register them.

Finally, there was much dissatisfaction with the agency's referral system, especially the lack of effective implementation of the Secretary of Labor's housing regulations of 1967, which prohibited the employment service from assisting the interstate recruitment of agricultural workers when housing furnished by the employer failed to meet minimum standards. The reviewers found that most of the demand states had taken measures to implement the Secretary's regulations, but the employment service commonly sent more workers to employers than they needed or ordered, causing housing to be inadequate. Moreover, despite efforts to improve housing, many farm workers continued to live in substandard housing because employers did not have to use the Rural Manpower Service in order to recruit labor.

As a consequence of the special review staff's findings, Secretary Hodgson directed a new program of reforms, including:

(1) The immediate consolidation of the Rural Manpower Service and the Labor Department's employment service to provide a "broader spectrum" of services to rural workers and employers

(2) Immediate action to eliminate discrimination and adopt procedures to ensure "full and continuing compliance" with civil rights laws

(3) Procedures to ensure compliance with child labor laws

(4) Effective enforcement of minimum wage laws

(5) Efforts to make sure that legally admitted foreign workers receive wages they are entitled to by law

(6) Measures to ensure that workers are provided adequate job and wage information about work they agree to do in the language they speak

(7) Steps to change civil service requirements to allow individuals with general farm experience, nonagricultural experience, and nonagricultural degrees to become eligible for positions in the employment service that serves rural and other residents

These and other charges against the Rural Manpower Service and the employment services were confirmed by the Federal District Court for the District of Columbia in the spring and summer of 1973. The court issued an injunction ordering Labor Department officials to "end any present participation in or perpetuation of discrimination and other unlawful practices against migratory and seasonal farmworkers" (*NAACP*, 1973). In June 1973, the Labor Department entered into a stipulation and agreement with the plaintiffs in this case to take corrective action and to institutionalize enforcement and monitoring functions to prevent future violations (*NAACP*, June 26, 1973). In August 1973, the court appointed a special master to "gather information that reflects the present capabilities" of the Labor Department to carry out the court's orders. This action was taken because plaintiffs continued to be dissatisfied with the Labor Department's efforts to correct the abuses complained of and to carry out its obligations under the stipulation and agreement.

The Monitor-Advocate System

During subsequent months, under federal court pressure, the Labor Department devoted considerable attention to implementing the Secretary's reforms. Each state employment service was directed to establish monitoring procedures (to ensure implementation of these reforms) and complaint procedures to facilitate prompt and fair resolution of complaints. These procedures were to be adopted in every state by July 1, 1974, and similar procedures were established at regional and national levels. The monitor-advocate system was to:

(1) Ensure that all complaints against employers, the employment service, or individual staff members are fairly and expeditiously handled. (This complaint procedure was not restricted to farm workers.)

(2) Make recommendations for corrective action to be taken at regional and national levels where complaints could not be resolved locally.

(3) Serve as general observation and monitoring agent to ensure the effectiveness of the monitor-advocate system.

(4) Serve as a "positive force" in encouraging necessary changes in the delivery of rural services.

According to the Labor Department's guidelines for setting up this system, the monitor-advocate would "fulfill a dual role"; as monitor, he would "observe and report to his administrator violations of directives and guidelines," and as advocate, he would "be a positive force in encouraging necessary changes in order to bring the organization and individuals in the organization into compliance."

The actions taken against the U.S. Employment Service apparently caused some corrective actions to be taken. As a result of an order from the Federal District Court in Washington, D.C., the employment service conducted on-site reviews of the Rural Manpower Service operations in fifteen states in July through September 1973. The reviews of 53 offices in these states revealed "some strengths and some weaknesses" in state and local office performance. However, the report of these visits concluded that the Secretary's reforms "are being implemented effectively" throughout all states that were visited. The report also found that no "substantial" difference existed between the "level of service provided to rural and urban workers or between farm workers and other workers." Moreover, the review did not "surface any pattern of discrimination in services" given minority applicants (including Spanish-surnamed applicants, "a goodly number of whom were migrants or ex-migrants").

Summary

Although it has shifted its emphasis, the Rural Manpower Service clearly has a long way to go before it changes its employer-oriented image. There are many reasons why it had difficulty shifting to a rural manpower service, the most obvious of which is the power of agribusiness interests relative to both the Rural Manpower Service and the workers. This agency has few sanctions; it seeks primarily to promote employer use of the employment service, but its main sanction against the employer is to deny him the use of those services.

Denial of the agency's services is a particularly impotent remedy when there are labor surpluses, or when labor market institutions have alternatives to the use of the employment service. Moreover, the narrow mission of the Farm Labor Service made it reasonably effective in meeting the employers' needs but made it very difficult to transform the Farm Labor Service's personnel and procedures into a true rural manpower service. Federal efforts in this direction are rendered even more difficult by the fact that the employment service has been controlled mainly by the states. Finally, farm workers' weaknesses make it difficult for them either to provide the necessary stimulus for change or to form an alternate constituency for the Rural Manpower Service.

CONCERTED SERVICES IN TRAINING AND EDUCATION

The program seems to have the basic ingredients of an effective rural development effort. In the first place, it concentrates on drawing together available resources in a community and therefore avoids the need for large additional public expenditures. Second, it relies on a local *coordinator*, appointed in each county by a statewide committee designated by the governor, to be the catalyst for development and therefore avoids rivalry among the participating agencies. Agencies are likely to accept a person who represents none of the other agencies more readily than they would a coordinator on loan from an established agency. The coordinator can take a more flexible approach in identifying existing and potential programs and opportunities, since he has no loyalties to particular groups or programs. Most of the coordinators are local residents, trained in human resource development, with a knowledge of local people and their resources and therefore able to work with them.

A third aspect, which gives the program considerable promise as a development procedure, is its heavy reliance on community involvement. To have any significant impact, a rural development program probably requires heavy reliance on harnessing community energy to identify goals, collect information, and otherwise support development programs. Development resources can be multiplied by relying on volunteers. For instance, industrial development often requires the collection of considerable labor market information, which sometimes has been done effectively by volunteers. An example of this was the Concerted Services in Training and Education program in Minnesota, which collected labor market information (on 11,211 people out of a work force of 17,838) that was used to attract industry. Smaller communities' mobile teams sufficiently flexible to complete a mail survey within two weeks helped with the survey.

Program coordinators are responsible for a variety of manpower and other activities to support economic development. Sometimes technical assistance is rendered to employers in order to make it possible for them to expand their employment. In other cases, program coordinators arrange financing to facilitate the establishment or survival of enterprises.

A November 1971 evaluation of the Concerted Services in Training and Education program concluded that the following lessons had been learned from the program as of that date:

(1) The county is the appropriate unit for program development purposes.

(2) The interagency approach is most effective.

(3) The coordinator's role of bringing together existing resources for development purposes is very important for development.

(4) Development requires the focusing of a variety of governmental services on particular projects.

(5) Development requires major emphasis on manpower development. According to McCauley (November 1971) : "It appears that the availability of training and education was sometimes a decisive factor in decisions by employers to locate in demonstration areas."

All of these conclusions seem valid, although the selection of the county as the appropriate unit for development purposes is valid only for the beginning of a program. Experience demonstrates the usefulness of expanding to neighboring counties to provide more latitude for development.

OPERATION MAINSTREAM*

Operation Mainstream, created in 1965 by the Nelson Amendment to the Economic Opportunity Act of 1964, has evolved into a collection of programs to provide public service employment for disadvantaged adult workers, a majority of whom live in rural areas. Congress intended for Operation Mainstream to be primarily an income maintenance program providing work for disadvantaged adult workers on community service projects, especially those which benefit the poor.

The intended target group was poor, older workers without access to other manpower programs in rural areas. Another stated objective of the program was to demonstrate that older workers are productive and capable of acquiring new skills. It was hoped that some enrollees could be placed in private, unsubsidized employment and also that private employers would be encouraged to change their hiring practices and hire a number of these workers. However, as we shall see, as Operation Mainstream evolved, the original concept was changed, especially in the newer components.

Operation Mainstream can be divided into two broad groups: (1) regional programs administered by the regional offices of the Labor Department through local contractors and (2) national programs administered by the Labor Department through contracts with five national organizations. The nationally contracted programs conform most

---

* This section is based on a paper by Webb, 1973.

closely to legislative intent. The participants in these programs are virtually all over 55 years of age and working on community service projects. Typically, there is little effort to train or to place enrollees outside the program. Enrollment in most national programs is not subject to a time limitation.

The regional programs emphasize placement of enrollees in permanent unsubsidized employment. The emphasis results in more training and less concern with community service and favors younger, more employable enrollees, and there usually is a maximum enrollment period ranging from three months to two years. However, most of the enrollees in Operation Mainstream, regional and national, live in rural areas.

*The Nationally Contracted Programs**

There are five Operation Mainstream programs contracted and monitored by the national office of the U.S. Training and Employment Service. These national programs are all essentially public service employment programs for the elderly poor, with virtually the same guidelines for enrollee eligibility: Enrollees must be at least 55 years old, have family income below the poverty guidelines, and have been either chronically unemployed or underemployed. The guidelines are generally well observed in the national programs. Almost all participants are over 55 years of age; the mean age for the national programs is about 66. The majority of enrollees meet the poverty and employment criteria, although some of the programs have sizable minorities of enrollees in violation of these guidelines.

Among the five national programs, there are essentially two models: the Green Thumb and the senior service programs — which includes the other four nationally contracted programs and the Green Light program. The Green Thumb program employs poor, elderly male workers in rural areas in physical improvement projects, working on parks, outdoor recreational facilities, and outdoor maintenance and clean-up crews. The Green Light (the female counterpart of Green Thumb) and the various senior service programs employ a majority of women in jobs with a service orientation; e.g., clerical aides, lunchroom aides, outreach workers for the elderly poor, and so forth. With the exception of Green Light and some local projects, most of the senior service programs are located in urban areas.

Since the national programs emphasize income maintenance and employment, they have no time limitation on enrollment. The Green

---

* This section is based on **Berry** *et al.*, January 1971 and May 1971.

Thumb-Green Light program is the oldest Operation Mainstream program (it began in 1966) and is larger than the rest of the nationally contracted programs combined. As of 1971, there were 2,407 Green Thumb-Green Light enrollees in seventeen state projects. This program, administered by the National Farmers Union through its state office, is simple: There are virtually no training, supportive services, placement, or follow-up activities. It effectively provides income maintenance for its target population, the elderly poor in rural areas, and some services to the community.

In contrast to Green Thumb's emphasis on physical beautification, the other four national programs are oriented toward service activities, typically with a majority of female enrollees.

The national contractors and their programs are as follows (numbers in parentheses are for 1972):

(1) The National Council of Senior Citizens which administers (5) below (nineteen projects, 1,148 enrollees)

(2) The National Council of Aging (eleven projects, 572 enrollees)

(3) The Senior Community Service project

(4) The National Retired Teachers Association (six projects, 353 enrollees)

(5) The Senior Community Aides project

(6) Virginia State College (one project, 125 enrollees)

(7) The Senior Community Service program

Although the eligibility guidelines are similar, the characteristics of participants in the various programs reflect the objectives of the contractors. The National Council of Aging programs give priority to services for elderly poor people. For example, the council had one rural project in an area with a high incidence of hunger to inform poor older people of food programs and other services for the indigent. However, the stress on serving elderly poor nonenrollees has resulted in substantial violations of eligibility criteria: 25 percent of the National Council of Aging enrollees were employed when entering the program, and 20 percent were over the poverty guideline.

The National Retired Teachers Association, which stresses placement (and is the only one of the nationally contracted Operation Mainstream programs to have a time limit on enrollment), adhered to eligibility guidelines, but it tended to serve middle-class people who became poor as they grew older. Consequently, by 1972 about 80 percent of this association's enrollees had worked in white-collar occupations and a fourth had worked in professional, managerial, and technical occupations. About half of the enrollees were black, and virtually all were urban and older than 55.

The federal costs per man-year of service run from $3,550 in Green Thumb to more than $5,000 in the other national programs, with the National Council of Aging program highest at $5,704. In all Operation Mainstream programs, more than 80 percent of federal costs represent wage and fringe benefit payments to enrollees (Berry *et al.*, *Phase IV*, p. 151). These costs contrast with an annual cost of about $9,000 for the Public Employment Program under the Emergency Employment Act.

Green Thumb in Texas*

Perhaps a review of the Texas Green Thumb program will provide a better understanding of Operation Mainstream's nature and limitations. Green Thumb in Texas provides work and income for poor, older, rural male residents. The program focuses mainly on income maintenance — through 1972, 80 percent of state Green Thumb funds were spent for wages and fringe benefits of the enrollees — and very little was provided for training, supportive services, or placement. The enrollees usually worked in racially integrated crews of seven on physical improvement projects for public and private nonprofit agencies, who supply the necessary materials and equipment.

Administratively, the state director of Green Thumb is in the state Farmers Union office in Waco. There are two field supervisors, one for eight panhandle-south plains counties and one for five central Texas counties.

Since there are many more potential Green Thumb enrollees than positions available, the program's administrators divide full-time positions among enrollees. For instance, in January 1972, a total of 209 enrollees shared 172 full-time slots. All of the enrollees were over 55 years of age, and 127 were over 62; there were 55 blacks, 37 chicanos, one Indian, and three women enrolled. Average annual preenrollment income was $1,100.

There was no systematic selection process for enrollees. Slots ordinarily were filled from among qualified applicants on a first-come, first-served basis. Crew foremen sometimes solicited applicants, but appli-

---

* This section is based on interviews with Texas Green Thumb enrollees and staff. Data are from the state Green Thumb office in Waco.

cants usually heard of the program by word-of-mouth and through other informal channels. Apparently very little effort was made to verify the statements on applications.

Although most enrollees are disadvantaged, there was one element of skimming in the Texas program. The crew foremen generally were younger and more skilled than other crew members. Some crew leaders could conceivably find other employment, although it is doubtful the crews could function without them. Ability to speak English appeared to be an informal requirement, and since the crews often were employed some distance from their homes, some potential participants who lacked transportation probably were excluded. Skimming also sometimes resulted from the use of program positions for political patronage.

The projects involved brush cutting, cleaning up, painting, concrete work, stone laying (for walls), making picnic benches, building playground equipment, and so forth. Host agencies included park departments, a church, a Boy Scout camp, juvenile detention centers, county commissioners, and a girls' home. The only kind of instruction (beyond safety training) was informal on-the-job training for minimal to moderate skill levels. Most of the projects involved building new facilities or improving old ones. Generally these facilities were not in poor neighborhoods. However, some of the work might violate the maintenance of effort clause; e.g., routine maintenance of county property. Because it creates a poor image in host communities, the Green Thumb staff sought to avoid the brush-cutting-type projects. Nevertheless, routine maintenance work sometimes was accepted to appease host agencies and to provide work for enrollees.

Very little was done to improve the employability of Green Thumb enrollees, and there was little turnover on the crews in the first two years the program operated in the central Texas area, and even the small amount of turnover was due to health or personal reasons and not to employment elsewhere. Also, there seemed to be little relationship between the Green Thumb project and public agencies capable of rendering supportive services to the program's participants.

In short, the Green Thumb project has effectively improved the incomes of a number of poor older workers, but other than the very significant improvement in the mental attitudes given the enrollees by working, the other needs of the enrollees — needs for supportive services, training, and placement — were largely ignored.

*Overview of Regional Operation Mainstream Programs**

The regionally contracted Operation Mainstream programs represent more than two-thirds of the total enrollment. These programs differ in three major respects from their national counterparts: administrative arrangements, characteristics of enrollees, and program goals. In the regional programs, the selection of local program sponsors is the responsibility of the regional manpower administrators. Although these administrators may in practice add to or modify program guidelines, the Labor Department merely monitors and does not supervise actual Operation Mainstream operations. The national eligibility guidelines are a minimum age of 22, family income below the poverty level, chronic unemployment or underemployment, and a minimum of 40 percent of enrollees older than 55.

There are two main types of regional programs: (1) projects which are part of Concentrated Employment Programs and (2) programs under the Economic Opportunity Act. The former had 2,052 Operation Mainstream enrollees in 42 local projects in 1971. Most of these programs were in urban areas. The latter had 8,490 enrollees in 310 primarily rural local programs in 1971.

Characteristics of enrollees vary considerably between individual programs, but in general the regional programs had younger enrollees; the mean age was about 41 or 42 years. The Concentrated Employment Programs in Operation Mainstream had mostly blacks, while the other regional programs had a majority of white enrollees. A national evaluation of the Concentrated Employment Programs of Operation Mainstream found the average age lower, incidence of possible guideline violations higher, and amount of training received somewhat less than in the Economic Opportunity Act programs (Berry *et al.*, August 1971, p. 15).

In contrast to the nationally contracted programs, the regional programs emphasize permanent placement in competitive employment as a primary goal and are not so concerned about community services. Regional program emphasis tends to cause the selection of younger, more employable applicants, the selection of work stations on the basis of training and placement opportunities rather than on potential community service, and the imposition of time limitations on enrollment (usually three months to two years).

---

* This section is based on Berry *et al.*, August 1971 and October 1971.

*The Public Employment Program**

The Public Employment Program initiated by the Emergency Employment Act of 1971 is like Operation Mainstream in that both are public employment programs and both have multiple and conflicting goals (Levitan and Taggart, June 1972, pp. 3–11). The program was designed to provide employment for unemployed workers and needed services to the public. It was supposed to help disadvantaged workers as well.

However, the Public Employment Program is clearly no substitute for Operation Mainstream in reaching the rural disadvantaged. Data on this and Operation Mainstream for 1972 reveal that 42 percent of Operation Mainstream enrollees and only 9 percent of Public Employment Program enrollees had eight years or less of school. At the other end of the scale, only 3 percent of Operation Mainstream enrollees, but 32 percent of Public Employment Program enrollees, had at least some college. Nationally, 73 percent of Operation Mainstream enrollees and 24 percent of public employment participants had less than a high school education. The same trend is evident at the state level: 43 percent of Texas public employment enrollees had some college, while less than 0.5 percent of Operation Mainstream enrollees had any college.** If education is a good measure of being disadvantaged, it would appear that Operation Mainstream serves a much larger proportion of disadvantaged workers.

A fairer comparison of Operation Mainstream and the Public Employment Program would be the latter's balance of state† vs regional Operation Mainstream in Texas. Cumulative enrollment figures for the first nine months of the Public Employment Program in Texas' balance of state support the conclusion that the public employment personnel were not so concerned as Operation Mainstream staff with disadvantaged workers. About 24 percent of Texas' balance-of-state enrollees had eight years or less of education, whereas only about 12 percent of Operation Mainstream enrollees in Texas were in the same group. Almost

---

* This section is based primarily on interviews conducted with district Manpower Administration staff, directors and staff of individual contractors, and data collected from the files of those contractors.

** Office of Manpower Management Data Systems, U.S. Department of Labor.

† "Balance of state" is the geographic area outside the political jurisdiction of other designated program agents participating in the Public Employment Program. These latter designated agents are primarily cities or counties of over 75,000 population which are directly funded. The balance of state is a residual consisting of smaller towns and rural areas. Balance-of-state funds are administered through the Department of Community Affairs, Office of the Governor, State of Texas.

60 percent of balance-of-state participants, but only 22 percent of those in Operation Mainstream, had twelve or more years of school. Only a fraction of 1 percent of Operation Mainstream enrollees in Texas had any education beyond high school, while 18.7 percent of the public employment balance-of-state enrollees had some college.*

According to the Public Employment Program's definition of "disadvantaged," 33.1 percent of balance-of-state enrollees were disadvantaged. Virtually all Operation Mainstream enrollees were disadvantaged by the same definition.

In the preliminary reports on the balance of state, 300 out of 1,500 public employment enrollees have been permanently placed. In contrast, the regional Operation Mainstream program with the best placement record placed about two-thirds of all terminees. Operation Mainstream apparently has skimmed less and has probably done as well or better in permanently placing enrollees. Of course, the Green Thumb program, which caters mainly to older workers, does not have as good a placement record as the Public Employment Program. Finally, the public employment program costs approximately $7,000 per enrollee, much higher than the cost per enrollee of Operation Mainstream.

Summary

The Green Thumb program is an effective low-cost income maintenance program providing income, work, and self-respect for poor older males in rural areas. The communities benefit from physical facilities and services.

The regional Operation Mainstream programs provide temporary income maintenance for needy persons as well as affording useful training and job development for some enrollees. They seek to reach a different target population (younger, more trainable) than the national Operation Mainstream programs. As contrasted with the Public Employment Program, the general programs do more for the disadvantaged, probably because they are administered by private organizations mainly interested in the disadvantaged. The regional programs probably can sustain at least as high a permanent placement rate as the Public Employment Program.

The inclusion of both older and younger workers in the same regional Operation Mainstream program is detrimental to both, since older

---

* The source of the Public Employment Program data is the Department of Community Affairs, Office of the Governor, State of Texas. The period covered is September 1, 1971, to March 31, 1972.

workers often need prolonged or permanent income maintenance and since the training needs of older and younger workers are different. The program carried out by the regional programs should continue since there is no apparent alternative for many of the enrollees. Other manpower programs will not even consider many of the Operation Mainstream enrollees as applicants due to their low levels of skill and educacation. The Public Employment Program enrollment is biased toward more highly qualified workers. In some of the isolated areas served, there are no alternatives to Operation Mainstream.

The experiences of the regional Operation Mainstream programs suggest some useful innovations in training methods. For example, combining on-the-job training and paid adult basic education classes appears to be a potentially very effective method of training. Crew projects can provide useful training if there is an incentive.

Most rural training programs suffer from lack of locally available jobs for completers. Creation of public employment is a partial solution. It seems conceivable that an Operation Mainstream program could complement the Public Employment Program and Public Service Careers programs in rural areas and small towns.

Multiple and conflicting goals and ambivalence on target groups have hampered the effectiveness of both the regional Operation Mainstream programs and the Public Employment Program. It would probably be better to have all older workers in Green Thumb-type programs and to let the regional Operation Mainstream programs concentrate on training. As presently constituted, none of the programs — regional Operation Mainstream, Public Employment Program, or Green Thumb — is likely to substantially change hiring practices as they apply to the disadvantaged poor.

The evidence suggests very strongly that a variety of public employment programs is needed for different target populations. While other types of public employment programs undoubtedly are needed for urban areas or to counteract generally rising levels of unemployment, Operation Mainstream has shown itself to be an effective and economical program to reach rural workers who have been displaced from agriculture but who are not likely to find private employment without intolerable levels of inflation. Not only can Operation Mainstream programs provide income and employment for rural residents, but many useful public services can be provided as well. The Texas experience indicates that Operation Mainstream programs could be easily expanded. For example, the director of one program had between six and ten applicants for each slot, and Green Thumb could easily be doubled in Texas.

THE START-UP TRAINING CONCEPT

The start-up training concept, adopted in a number of states during the 1960s and 1970s, is designed to overcome some of the main weaknesses of traditional manpower and vocational training programs; namely, the absence of jobs for people who have been trained, the difficulties in gearing training precisely to the needs of particular employers, and the fact that prospective employers often encounter considerable uncertainty as to the availability of qualified workers in places where they contemplate establishing plants. The start-up training concept attempts to minimize these problems by using training as an inducement to industrialization; it is based on the assumption that high-wage industry can be induced to hire workers in a particular place only if those workers possess the skills to give them the productivity to command higher wages.

Under this concept, the employer's prospective work force is carefully selected and trained before the plant actually opens. The relevancy of the training can be assured by having it supervised by the plant's prospective supervisory personnel, who can even be hired by the state as instructors for this purpose. The relevancy of training also is assured by having the employees use the same kinds of equipment for training purposes that they are likely to use on the job.

Start-up training programs are under way in a number of states, but the concept has not yet been carefully evaluated anywhere (such an evaluation currently is being undertaken at the Center for the Study of Human Resources, University of Texas), although South Carolina's program is generally regarded as "the" model. This program is supposed to have significantly accelerated the location of supramarginal industry in that state. South Carolina officials also have sought to plan the location of industry within the state to match the industry with the characteristics of local residents through a computerized labor market information system. The South Carolina program also utilizes a systems approach to training and a network of technical training centers throughout the state.

The late Wade Martin, one of the originators of the South Carolina program, considered it important to separate the technical training program from academic educational institutions in order to make training more responsive to industry needs and to avoid academic restrictions on programs and the selection of instructors. However, the South Carolina program has become more integrated with the academic education system since Martin's death.

ADEQUACY OF MANPOWER OUTLAYS IN RURAL AREAS

Manpower expenditures, like most other social outlays, have had an urban bias. As Table 4-4 indicates, rural areas receive a less than proportionate share of human resource program funds, except for elementary and secondary education. In part, this is because the problems of urban areas are more conspicuous, and the cities have more proposal-writing and administrative expertise. Except for agribusiness interests, which have had very little interest in human resource development programs, rural residents also have not been very well organized politically. As a consequence, most rural residents apparently know nothing about manpower services. For example, a paper by the Rural Manpower Service office of the Atlanta regional manpower administrator's office (which has a major concern for rural manpower development) concludes: "Manpower services systems have largely been concentrated in urban areas. Rural residents, more frequently than not, are not aware

Table 4-4

Federal Human Resource Program Expenditures in
Nonmetropolitan Areas
(Fiscal year 1969; millions of dollars)

Program	Actual	If Proportionate to Population	Gap
Health facilities construction	$ 155	$ 169	$ 14
Health services and care	808	1,092	284
Elementary and secondary education	844	787	– 57
Higher and science education	377	436	59
Vocational education and manpower training	196	316	120
TOTAL	$2,380	$2,800	$420

SOURCE: *Locational Analysis of Federal Expenditures in Fiscal Year 1969,* Evaluation Division, Office of Management and Budget (September 1, 1970).

of the existence of a Federal State Employment system. Service to most rural areas is non-existent." *

By whatever standard we judge manpower experiences, the evidence seems to support the conclusion that rural areas have been shortchanged in manpower efforts. An issue paper prepared by the Labor Department (*Rural Manpower*) concluded that rural areas, with 22 percent of the population in 1969, received about 6.9 percent of labor and manpower outlays. The paper gives estimates for 1969 as shown in Table 4-5. Thus while the rural universe of need for manpower programs accounts for one-third of the total, less than one-fourth of the enrollees were in rural areas (see Table 4-6 for comparable expenditure levels for non-SMSAs). In 1971, a strategy paper produced by the Rural Manpower Service estimated that 23 percent of manpower outlays were in rural areas, which had 31 percent of the population and a larger proportion of all poor persons. Moreover, it was estimated that the rural employment service staff constituted about 16 percent of the total (Manpower Administration, June 1971).

The Rural Manpower Service strategy paper identified a number of obstacles to effective manpower planning for rural areas, including: (1) program inflexibility, which causes (a) the unique needs of rural people to be ignored and (b) a preoccupation with perpetuating a bureaucracy rather than encouraging innovation and "sometimes leads to inappropriate attempts to fit urban models to rural situations," and (2) poor coordination, which causes interagency coordination often to

TABLE 4-5

Estimates of Labor and Manpower Outlays
(1969)

Category	Total	Million Urban	Rural
Universe of need*	9.200	6.200	3.000
Enrollees	1.033	0.786	0.247

* The percentage of enrollment of the universe of need was 11, 13, and 8, respectively.
SOURCE: *Rural Manpower*, Issue Paper No. 5, U.S. Department of Labor.

---

* I am indebted to William Norwood, Jr., regional manpower administrator for the Atlanta region, for a copy of the paper, "Problems and Perplexities of Rural People."

TABLE 4-6

Major Federal Manpower Programs and Share
in Non-SMSAs
(Fiscal year 1970)

Agency and Program	Percentage of Total in Non-SMSA	Total (millions of dollars)
U.S. Department of Labor:		
On-the-job training	14.4%	$ 25.4*
MDTA institutional training	16.7	92.9*
Placement Services Administration	18.9	155.6*
Concentrated Employment Program	9.3	50.6*
Job Opportunities in the Business Sector	8.5	65.0*
Neighborhood Youth Corps	36.8	99.7*
Work Incentive Program	1.1	16.4*
New Careers	8.3	5.3*
Operation Mainstream	72.7	26.0*
Job Corps	40.8	41.7*
SUBTOTAL	22.8	578.7*
U.S. Department of Health, Education and Welfare:		
Manpower Development and Training	9.2	154.7

* First half of fiscal year 1970 only.
SOURCE: Joseph D. Coffey, "Rural Manpower: Program Needs, Payoffs, Delivery, and Direction," talk presented to the National Agricultural Outlook Conference (Washington, D.C., 1971), Table 5.

be characterized by "lip service" instead of meaningful action and perpetuates "spheres of influence concerning program prerogatives."

In order to assure equity, the Rural Manpower Service recommended earmarking funds for use in rural areas in at least the ratio of the rural to total population (22 percent) by the Labor Department's definition and preferably the ratio of the rural percentage of poverty (32 percent). The Rural Manpower Service paper also advocated innovative measures to develop manpower programs specifically designed for rural areas, and planning for flexibility in order to permit regional adaptations of rural manpower policy, involvement of local community leadership in adapting programs to local realities, and special attention to the problems of rural minorities.

In addition to the appointment of rural manpower advocates at the national and regional levels, the paper recommended training and reorientation to permit farm labor personnel to become "manpower development specialists with a special appreciation for the manpower problems of rural areas."

It is not clear whether funds either should or should not be earmarked for rural areas, but the suggestion deserves careful consideration. Probably the greatest arguments for such an allocation are the intensity of need and the probability that the powerlessness of rural workers will make it unlikely that they can exert enough political pressure to get fair treatment in the absence of some arbitrary allocation.

Another manpower issue involves the place to train rural workers. Some argue that because of the absence of institutional and on-the-job training facilities in rural areas, training must take place in urban areas. Others, like Hathaway, argue that it should take place in rural areas (if employment expansion is the objective) in order to permit training to be coordinated with economic development activities (May 1971, p. 13).

Evidence from a careful study of relocation projects in Michigan and Wisconsin suggests that migrants benefit very little from training, although nonmigrants are helped considerably by it. This issue cannot be resolved because it depends on the circumstances and the objectives of the manpower programs. If more manpower programs are devoted to training agricultural workers, for example, as perhaps they should be, training might take place in rural areas or perhaps at the manufacturers' factories. Moreover, if local authorities wanted to use training as an adjunct of economic development, they could provide local training institutions for that purpose.

RELOCATION ASSISTANCE

Measures to relocate workers from labor surplus to labor shortage areas have become important parts of the manpower policies of many countries, particularly Sweden, Great Britain, and Canada (Jenness, 1969). These countries offer relocation for workers who are unemployed or underemployed. Programs are not necessarily limited to depressed areas, but in Britain and Sweden, 80 percent of the participants are from areas of high unemployment. Canada offers assistance to any unemployed or underemployed worker who has a permanent job offer in another community. European relocation programs ordinarily are administered by employment services.

Because natural migration patterns have not been sufficient to reduce surplus populations in many rural areas or to reduce income inequalities within agriculture or between agriculture and other sectors (McDonald, 1971; Fuller, 1970), there is considerable support for relocation programs as better alternatives than fruitless attempts to attract industry to rural areas with little economic potential, transfer payments, or a continuation of the economically "irrational" migration patterns based mainly on information and assistance from friends, relatives, and other contacts, rather than where job opportunities are best (Hansen, 1970 and 1971). Those who favor "growth center strategies" advocate programs to rationalize the labor market by making it possible for people to move to these growth centers rather than to congested urban areas.

As a consequence of this reasoning, MDTA provided for a number of relocation assistance projects which afford some insight into the effectiveness of this strategy. These pilot projects moved some fourteen thousand unemployed and underemployed workers and their families, mainly from the rural areas, between 1965 and 1969, at a cost of approximately $800 per family, including about $300 for moving and getting settled. These projects were generally regarded as successful in moving the unemployed and underemployed to new jobs. These programs also made it possible to isolate some key factors facilitating mobility, including the need for a wide range of supportive services and the value in tying those who are relocated to specific jobs before they make the move.

As with all experimental operations, results of the relocation effort were mixed. There appears to have been a strong commitment to the need for a flexible project-by-project approach in implementing relocation activities. Different services were required for successful relocation of low-skilled rural workers, compared to well-trained technical personnel displaced by mass layoffs in urban areas. In the case of the low skilled, basic education should have generally preceded any attempt at relocation, and an extensive array of supportive services before and after the move appears to have been essential. On the other hand, assistance in locating jobs from a distance or financial aid was all that was necessary for displaced skilled and professional people. The relocation of low-skilled workers is obviously of higher priority, especially since many well-trained workers would move without assistance.

Relocation Costs

Although some workers were willing to move without financial aid, nine out of ten received financial aid for: (1) moving expenses and in some situations for temporary storage of household goods, (2) lump sum allowances, which were determined by the average weekly factory worker's pay, to the worker and his spouse and half that amount each for up to four dependents, and (3) temporary dual-household subsistence payments to enable workers to try a new job and to arrange housing before moving their families.

The lump sum living allowances were more than half the average cost; 30 percent was for the transportation and storage of household goods, and 20 percent was for travel allowances. The highest costs were for skilled workers moving longer distances, requiring higher average transportation costs. Unskilled workers tended to move shorter distances (84 percent of all moves were for less than five hundred miles) but required more extensive supportive services.

The relocation projects were opposed by community leaders in rural areas where growers resisted the relocation of their labor supply, whether underemployed or unemployed during an off season. Resistance was particularly strong to attempts to relocate younger, more productive workers and those with more skills, experience, or education.

A careful evaluation of MDTA experimental relocation projects in Michigan and Wisconsin by Somers (1972) provides some additional and more specific insights into the uses and limitations of this approach. The Michigan-Wisconsin projects moved people from northwest Wisconsin mainly to Milwaukee and larger Wisconsin towns and from three counties in the upper peninsula of Michigan mainly to Detroit and other larger Michigan cities. To be eligible, workers had to be unemployed and have a job offer which gave promise of permanent employment in the demand communities. Participants were given loans which were turned into grants if they remained six months on the new job, became involuntarily unemployed, or found another job within commuting distance of the new residence. The program provided grants for transportation and various supportive services.

Somers and his associates surveyed 305 workers six months after they had relocated. In Wisconsin, these people were compared with a random sample of 347 workers from groups who were willing and eligible but did not move, another group who said they definitely did not want to move, a third made up of people who indicated a willingness to move under certain conditions, and a fourth drawn at random from employment service files. The Michigan comparison groups consisted of 384 trainees who had enrolled in the Marquette Area Training Center but who did not relocate.

The Michigan-Wisconsin project led to several conclusions:

(1) Although there was a similar age pattern between movers and the 19 percent of the relocated who returned to their home areas, as compared with nonmovers, those who moved were younger, more likely to be male, and high school graduates. Two-thirds were married.

(2) The employment positions of movers improved more markedly after the moves than those of either nonmovers or returnees. All three groups had similar earnings before the move, but movers' earnings had increased significantly within six months.

(3) Surprisingly, MDTA training apparently had relatively little impact on earnings after the move; however, nonmovers with training had higher earnings than nonmovers without training.

(4) Although the movers generally improved their incomes relative to the other two groups, they were not satisfied with their moves after six months; they were more interested in further moves than nonmovers and wanted to move back home.

(5) The success of movers was associated with city size. A larger percentage of the movers to cities of over 250,000 population returned to their home areas than was true of those who moved to cities of 25,000 to 249,000. However, the samples from various-sized cities were too small to support generalizations on this point.

Somers concluded from his analysis that relocation projects could overcome the obstacles to mobility among many unemployed and underemployed workers in economically depressed areas. In general, moving costs were important but probably not a significant barrier to movement. The nonfinancial supportive assistance (counseling, housing, and so forth) probably was more important. The Michigan-Wisconsin projects suggest that relocation is a sound social investment but that there are large social and psychological costs of moving which must be considered. Moreover, Somers' analysis questions the value of training relocatees before they are moved and, although there were not enough data for a conclusive answer to this question, emphasizes the value of inducing migration to cities with populations between 25,000 and 249,000, rather than to cities larger than that. Finally, Somers argues, relocation alone cannot solve the problems of depressed areas and must therefore be used in conjunction with other programs.

Somers' findings of the social and psychological costs of moving are important because they have implications for the acceptance of relocation and the effects on migration of various public policies, especially measures to provide general income maintenance. Unfortunately, we have little reliable information on the noneconomic factors in mobility, but there is evidence that these factors are very important in many cases (Price, 1969; Turner, 1949; Fairchild, 1970).

Migration is influenced by where people want to live, but we have very little information concerning preferences under various conditions. We have some evidence that black rural youth prefer to live in urban areas, at least under the historical conditions prevailing in the rural South. For example, a study of rural high school youths in three east Texas counties found that 63 percent of them wanted to live in large cities as compared with only 16 percent of white youths (Kuvlesky and Pelham, June 1970, pp. 166–76). A Florida study reached similar conclusions (Youmans *et al.*, 1965). There probably has been a long-term historical preference for urban living by blacks and whites.

However, there is some indication that the general public's preference for urban places underwent considerable change during the 1960s and early 1970s. Two national surveys conducted during the summer of 1972 found that eight out of ten people polled would prefer to live in suburban or rural areas if they had a choice, though most of those who prefer rural places prefer places within driving distance of cities. A Gallup poll released in December 1972 found that only 13 percent of the 1,457 adults interviewed in three hundred localities thought the city was an ideal place to live. Indeed only 20 percent of those who lived in cities at the time of the survey said they preferred city life. In a 1966 Gallup poll, 36 percent of city residents preferred city life (Rosenthal, 1972).

Similarly, a survey of 1,806 adults conducted for Potomac Associates during the summer of 1972 found that 36 percent of those surveyed lived in cities, but that only 18 percent preferred to live there. Only 18 percent of those in the Potomac Associates survey lived in rural areas, but 38 percent wished they did. The Gallup poll found the preference for non-urban life to be strongest among blue-collar families in the East with growing children. The findings in the Potomac Associates survey are presented in Table 4-7. Although these polls provide some insight into locational preferences, their usefulness is limited for mobility purposes because they do not provide information on the costs people are willing to incur in order to live in the preferred places.

Conclusion

Between 1965 and 1969, the relocation projects, after screening forty thousand eligible workers, assisted some fourteen thousand in actual moves. Nine out of ten were men; 60 percent had dependents; 80 percent were white; one-half were between 25 and 44 years of age, with one-third under 25. Although one-fourth had elementary education or less, half had graduated from high school. Most movers had been unemployed for some time or were farm workers earning under $1,200 per year. Sixty percent moved less than three hundred miles, and only a fifth, mostly skilled defense workers, moved more than five hundred miles. Nearly 60 percent of the moves were to cities under 250,000 population; only 10 percent went to major metropolitan areas.

Although these projects might have other objectives, success required that the movers (1) remain in the new locations and (2) improve their conditions there. The Labor Department reported that only 20 percent returned home two months after the move, with 20 percent of those who remained changing jobs during the first two months. However, an independent examination found about a third of the movers to have returned to the point of origin within sixty days, with only a third to a fifth remaining with their original jobs (E. F. Shelley and Company, Inc., 1969). The Labor Department reported an improvement in retention

TABLE 4-7

Present Residence and Preferred Residence
(Survey of 1,806 adults, 1972)

Category	Present Residence	Preferred Residence
City	36%	18%
Suburb	22	22
Town or village	15	19
Rural area	18	38
Unsure of place	9	3

SOURCE: Potomac Associates, Washington, D.C., reported in New York *Times* (November 17, 1972).

from 70 percent in 1965 projects to 88 percent in 1968. However, the success of relocation clearly depends on economic conditions in the receiving areas. During the 1970–71 period, for example, many of those who had been "successfully" placed lost their jobs.

There seems to be general agreement that the results were favorable for those who did remain in their new locations (Fairchild, 1969; Freedman, 1968), where their employment was more stable and their earnings higher than control groups who remained behind. Relocation costs for those who remained in their new location were soon recouped, but it is doubtful that the gains for those who remained were sufficient to offset the costs of those who returned home. Skilled workers had a higher propensity to move than others and were more likely to stay with their new jobs. Unskilled workers found it difficult to obtain jobs and to take advantage of the program. When relocation was combined with basic education and skills training, willingness to move was higher and the return rate lower. MDTA graduates and those with larger numbers of dependents were more willing to move than others.

The rate of return was primarily determined by such noneconomic factors as kinfolk ties, climate, school system, and general living problems. Layoffs, job losses, and declining employment opportunities in the demand areas were often followed by a return to the home area. In general, skilled workers tended to maintain their wage rates; those with industrial experience usually received higher pay than had been their supply area experience. Unskilled rural workers tended to receive the federal minimum wage.

The projects' main influence probably was to affect the timing and destination of the moves. In unaided moves, kinship and ethnic patterns are apparently more important determining factors than economic opportunity. Migrants tend to move to where others such as they have already moved, increasing concentrations of low-skilled workers where an oversupply already exists. The relocation projects increased the economic rationality of the moves. Many of the demand areas showed remarkable ability to absorb workers with limited skills, although the most disadvantaged often had trouble finding and keeping jobs.

The proportion of those in rural areas who were eligible for the programs who said they wanted to move was small. Those for whom, on objective grounds, the need for relocation was greatest were the most reluctant to move. Financial assistance apparently encouraged mobility and probably was even more important in the retention rate. The lump sum living allowance bridged the difficult time until the first wages were paid. As important as the financial assistance was, however, the availability of jobs and help in overcoming the problems involved in moving and resettling were more crucial.

The experiences of relocation projects were generally favorable, although we do not have enough information for definitive conclusions. The successes were low cost, but the overall result depends upon more information than is available on the proportions of retentions and returnees and on the effects of relocation on supply areas, especially if relocation efforts were expanded and made into permanent programs. Some of those assisted probably would have moved on their own in the absence of the program, but the limited resources available to the most disadvantaged would have made the costs of moving a serious financial burden for them (for further discussion, see *Symposium on the Role of Worker Relocation*, 1969).

Despite their apparent success, however, relocation programs have a number of limitations which make it hard to sell them to policy makers. One of these is the difficulty in being certain that people who are assisted by these projects are not those who would have moved in any case. In spite of limitations, the projects assisted mainly the kinds of people who already were the most mobile. Why, it might be asked, should scarce manpower money be used to support people who would move anyway? Moreover, it is not at all clear that many of those who are immobile would benefit more from relocation than from the creation of jobs close to their current location. After all, many workers with limited education and work experience are likely to work in marginal jobs or return to rural areas even if they are relocated. Moreover, the relocation of more productive workers has a detrimental effect on the economic potential of the supply areas which must be balanced against the gains to the mover. Finally, the relocation projects also face opposition from politicians who do not want to see their districts depopulated.

Better job information and some form of income maintenance might accelerate present migration trends. By removing the financial risks, younger, better educated workers might move more readily. On the other hand, the lower costs of living in rural areas might cause some income maintenance recipients to return to rural areas. Although there is very limited information on rural-urban cost-of-living differentials, the evidence available suggests that in some cases they are as large as 100 percent (Watts, 1969, p. 10, Table 1).

There seems to be a growing preference for rural and small town living in the United States which could further increase the reluctance of many workers to accept relocation assistance and could accelerate movements to rural areas and smaller towns, especially if there were job opportunities there. However, preference polls like those conducted for Potomac Associates and by Gallup might not be too meaningful for actual decision making because they do not indicate the costs of living in smaller communities in terms of employment opportunities. There is considerable evidence that people will sacrifice earnings in order to remain in and return to small towns and rural areas, but there is nevertheless continuing net outmigration because of inadequate job opportunities in those areas. Given the preferences for rural areas, however, economic conditions would not have to be equalized to hold rural populations or to attract returnees.

In conclusion, the evidence suggests that relocation assistance could be an important component of manpower policy, especially for younger, better educated workers. Those who benefit from relocation are the ones who have the greatest tendency to migrate without assistance, raising a question about the net effects of relocation assistance. Probably, however, the main effect of this assistance is to affect the timing and destination of moves, which is not unimportant. A major benefit of the projects for all groups, especially the disadvantaged, was to provide better information about jobs and living conditions in the alternate places to which people might relocate. The counseling and supportive services probably are more important, especially to low-income groups, than the financial assistance with moves. There is conflicting evidence on the value of training before moves. Many manpower and development specialists consider training to be an important determinant of successful moves, but Somers' study of the Michigan-Wisconsin relocatees found training to be insignificant. Even among younger, more mobile groups, there seems to be considerable social and psychological costs of moving which, combined with economic difficulties in urban areas, cause considerable back movement. Measuring the gains and losses from migration is inherently difficult because it is practically impossible to hold other things constant, cost-of-living differentials tend to be ignored, and noneconomic costs cannot be measured. The studies that have been made could have been improved, however, if they had included successful and unsuccessful moves in their cost calculations and had a follow-up of movers at succeeding intervals after they moved. The Labor Department's measurements two months after moves clearly did not allow enough time for success to be evaluated, especially in view of the large back movements found in studies longer times after relocation.

Finally, there is considerable political opposition to relocating, which could be minimized by keeping the moves within states and keeping the distances moved as short as possible.

RURAL EDUCATION

The educational levels of people in rural areas by race are shown in Table 4-8. The education of rural whites lags far behind that of their counterparts in metropolitan areas, but blacks are particularly disadvantaged. Indeed about three-fourths of all rural blacks had less than eight years of schooling in 1970.

For employment purposes, there is an urgent need to improve rural vocational education. In this connection, the area vocational schools,

TABLE 4-8

Educational Attainment of Persons
25 Years and Older by Race
(1970)

	Percentage of Population with			
	Eight Years of School or Less		Twelve Years of School or More	
Age and Residence	White	Black	White	Black
Total, 25 years and over:	26.1%	43.0%	57.4%	33.7%
Metropolitan areas	22.1	36.0	61.5	38.8
Nonmetropolitan areas	33.2	60.9	50.0	20.6
Nonfarm	31.7	59.1	51.2	21.6
Farm	43.1	74.5	42.0	11.9
25 to 44 years:	11.8	22.4	71.6	47.9
Metropolitan areas	9.4	18.0	74.7	52.2
Nonmetropolitan areas	16.5	36.3	65.9	34.2
Nonfarm	15.9	34.3	66.2	35.3
Farm	21.8	54.1	62.3	23.7
45 years and over:	36.8	63.1	46.6	19.9
Metropolitan areas	32.1	55.7	51.2	24.2
Nonmetropolitan areas	44.9	78.9	38.7	10.5
Nonfarm	43.4	77.9	40.0	11.3
Farm	53.5	86.4	31.9	4.6

SOURCE: Bureau of the Census, U.S. Department of Commerce.

which supplement vocational offerings in rural schools, seem particularly promising. These schools were provided for by the Vocational Education Act of 1963 and have done a great deal to train rural people for nonagricultural jobs.

Rural education faces a number of difficulties in addition to the problems involved in serving scattered populations, especially the inadequate education resources. Moreover, rural schools have not served minority groups very well, especially in the South, and have concentrated a disproportionate share of their resources on traditional agricultural subjects, while inadequately preparing people for nonfarm jobs.

It is doubtful that rural areas will be able to finance education systems that will put their people on a par with those of urban areas. Since this is a problem affecting the whole country, the federal government should explore means of providing minimum educational support.

SUMMARY AND CONCLUSIONS

This chapter has demonstrated something of the need and potential for manpower programs in rural areas. It is difficult to conceive of an effective rural development strategy that would not contain a sizable manpower component, whether that strategy were designed to facilitate the adjustment of people from declining industries to growth sectors or areas, to relocate people from labor surplus areas, to facilitate economic development, or to create public service jobs for those not likely to be absorbed in the private sector or those not likely to benefit from relocation.

Despite this potential, however, a number of factors in rural labor markets have limited human resource development. For one thing, dominant agribusiness groups have had limited interest in human resource development because their manpower requirements have mainly been for unskilled labor. However, this is changing as technological developments in agriculture increase the skill requirements of agricultural workers and as the growth of nonfarm industry erodes the influence of agribusiness. Unfortunately, however, too many rural industries are marginal operations not much more interested in education and training than agribusiness. On the other hand, heavy outmigration from many rural labor markets and the growth of welfare programs to create alternatives to work at very low wages have caused agricultural employers to pay more attention to manpower and labor markets. Many even realize the need for increasing wages and social benefits in order to hold the more productive workers in their geographic areas. Similarly, many rural public officials realize the need for developing and maintaining their work forces in order to attract industry and raise the incomes of their constituents.

The development of effective rural manpower programs is impeded by other characteristics of rural labor markets. Many manpower programs have been developed in response to urban problems and therefore are not adaptable to rural conditions. For example, the typical farm operator derives most of his income from off-farm work, but there are very few manpower programs to help small farmers upgrade their farming capabilities and acquire nonfarm skills to improve off-farm earnings.

There are, however, some experimental programs that have at least partially demonstrated their effectiveness as instruments for rural human resource development. These include Operation Hitchhike, Concerted Services in Training and Education, Area Concept Expansion, Operation Mainstream, start-up training, and Neighborhood Youth Corps. These programs could be perfected, enlarged, and adapted to the unique characteristics of rural labor markets.

Finally, inadequate allocations of funds also make it difficult to develop rural manpower programs. A notable characteristic of every rural manpower program is the small, and even insignificant, number of enrollees relative to the universe of need. The present level of rural manpower effort can only be justified in terms of experimentation, and some of these experiments have demonstrated their utility. Because of the rural leadership problem, a combination of community coordinators of the Concerted Services in Training and Education type on a multiple-county planning area basis and formula allocations of funds to rural areas would be more appropriate than present arrangements. Funds might be allocated on the basis of a subemployment index similar to the one calculated in chapter 3. This presupposes, of course, that there is an adequate national manpower effort, which has not been the case.

REFERENCES

Berry, Dale W.; *et al. National Evaluation of Operation Mainstream.* Phases I through IV. Washington, D.C.: Kirschner Associates, Inc. January, May, August, October (*Supplement*), and December 1971.

E. F. Shelley and Company, Inc. *Labor Mobility Study.* Progress Report No. 2. New York: E. F. Shelley and Company, Inc. June 1969.

Fairchild, Charles K. "Subsidized Relocation of the Rural Unemployed: Benefits and Costs." Paper presented to the Southern Economic Association, November 14, 1969.

————. *Worker Relocation: A Review of U.S. Department of Labor Mobility Demonstration Projects.* Washington, D.C.: E. F. Shelley and Company, Inc. 1970.

Freedman, Audrey. "Labor Mobility Projects for the Unemployed." *Monthly Labor Review* (June 1968).

Fuller, Varden. *Rural Worker Adjustment to Urban Life.* Ann Arbor, Michigan: Institute of Labor and Industrial Relations, University of Michigan-Wayne State University, and National Manpower Policy Task Force. 1970.

Griessman, B. Eugene. *Planned Change in Low-Income Rural Areas: An Evaluation of Concerted Services in Training and Education.* Raleigh: North Carolina State University, Center for Occupational Education. 1969.

Hansen, Niles. "Growth Centers, Human Resources, and Rural Development." In *Human Resource Development in the Rural South.* Final report to the Office of Economic Opportunity. Austin: University of Texas, Center for the Study of Human Resources. Mimeographed. 1971.

————. *Rural Poverty and the Urban Crisis.* Bloomington: University of Indiana Press. 1970.

Hathaway, Dale. "The Manpower Challenge in Rural Areas." *Rural Manpower Developments* (May 1971).

Jenness, Robert A. "Manpower Mobility Programs." Proceedings of a North American conference on cost-benefit analysis of manpower policies. Kingston, Ontario, Industrial Relations Centre, 1969.

Kuvlesky, William P.; and Pelham, John T. "Place of Residence Projections of Rural Youth: A Racial Comparison." *Social Science Quarterly* (June 1970).

Levitan, Sar A.; and Taggart, Robert. "The Emergency Employment Act: An Interim Assessment." *Monthly Labor Review* (June 1972), vol. 95, no. 6.

Manpower Administration, Rural Manpower Service. *A Rural Manpower Strategy.* Washington, D.C.: U.S. Department of Labor. June 1971.

————, Special Review Staff. *Review of the Rural Manpower Service.* Washington, D.C.: U.S. Department of Labor. 1972.

————. *A Rural Manpower Strategy.* Washington, D.C.: U.S. Department of Labor. June 1971.

McCauley, John S. "Concerted Services." *Rural Manpower Develop-ments* (September-October 1971).

————. "Problems Related to Improving the Organization of Train-ing in Small Towns and Rural Areas." Paper presented to the Na-tional Manpower Advisory Committee, November 1971.

McDonald, Stephen L. "Economic Factors in Farm Outmigration: A Survey and Evaluation of the Literature." In *Human Resource De-velopment in the Rural South.* Edited by Ray Marshall. Final re-port to the Office of Economic Opportunity (LG-6994). Austin: University of Texas, Center for the Study of Human Resources. 1971.

NAACP, WESTERN REGION *et al.* vs PETER J. BRENNAN *et al.* Civil Action No. 2010-72, U.S. District Court, District of Columbia (May 3, 1973, and June 26, 1973).

New York *Times*, April 23, 1972.

Price, Daniel O.; *et al. A Study of the Economic Consequences of Rural-to-Urban Migration.* Austin, Texas: Tracor, Inc. 1969.

Rosenthal, Jack. "Nonurban Living Is Gaining Favor." New York *Times.* December 17, 1972.

Rural Manpower. Issue Paper No. 5. U.S. Department of Labor.

Somers, Gerald G. *Labor Mobility: An Evaluation of Pilot Projects in Michigan and Wisconsin.* Madison: University of Wisconsin, In-dustrial Relations Research Institute. 1972.

Symposium on the Role of Worker Relocation in an Active Manpower Policy. Agency for International Development and U.S. Depart-ment of Labor. Washington, D.C., April 9 through 11, 1969.

Turner, Ralph. "Migration to a Medium-Sized City." *Journal of Social Psychology* (1949), vol. 80.

Watts, Harold W. *The Measurement of Poverty — An Exploratory Exercise.* Reprint No. 42. Madison: University of Wisconsin, Insti-tute for Research on Poverty. 1969.

Webb, James L. "Operation Mainstream in Central and South Texas." Austin: University of Texas, Center for the Study of Human Re-sources. 1973. Mimeographed.

Youmans, E. Grant; *et al. After High School, What . . . .* University of Florida, Cooperative Extension Service. 1965.

5. Rural Organizations

A MAJOR PROBLEM for rural development has been the virtual absence of organizations to represent small farmers, agricultural workers, and low-income groups in general. The weakness of these groups has caused them to be neglected by public policy and unable to protect their economic interests. Indeed even those inadequate protective and welfare measures that have been adopted often are not adequately enforced or are violated because there are no organizations controlled by low-income groups to protect their interests before, and file complaints with, administrative bodies. The few organizations that have been established often have been able to accomplish a great deal with meager resources. We also have noted that the absence of organizations makes it difficult to extend manpower and other human resource activities to rural areas.

The social ferment of the 1960s activated two organizations with considerable promise as agencies to represent the interests of small farmers and rural workers: cooperatives and unions, both of which concentrated initially on the problems of agricultural workers and small farmers but came to have wider interests. In addition, community development corporations were formed which also addressed themselves to the varied economic and social problems of rural workers. This chapter appraises the activities of these organizations and attempts to assess their future prospects.

Low-Income Cooperatives and Economic Development

Cooperatives have a long history as organizations to permit individuals to engage in various collective undertakings. Indeed cooperatives seem to be such natural enterprises that they exist in one form or another in every kind of economic system and under a variety of circumstances. Because they are democratic organizations controlled by their members and designed primarily to benefit their members, cooperatives have been highly regarded as ideal self-help organizations. It is therefore not surprising that in the social ferment of the 1960s, those interested in the problems of race, poverty, and economic development should have turned to cooperatives as organizational devices to help solve the problems of the poor, especially in rural areas.

Nature of Cooperatives

Cooperatives have the following characteristics:

(1) They are owned and controlled by their member-customers on a democratic basis. Each member usually has one vote, but in some cases votes are allocated to members on the basis of patronage. This distinguishes co-ops from corporations, which allocate control and voting rights in proportion to the capital invested by stockholders, who may or may not be customers of the firm.

(2) Cooperatives also differ from other businesses in the manner in which surplus earnings are distributed. The co-op's net receipts over costs are returned to customers in proportion to their patronage and not in proportion to their capital investment. These returns are called "patronage refunds." This technique usually enables members and patrons to obtain goods or services at lower prices and to sell their goods to others at higher prices than would be possible if they bought from or sold to private traders. Indeed cooperatives would have great difficulty surviving unless they provided terms at least as favorable to their members as those available from private traders.

(3) Membership in a cooperative is voluntary. Co-ops are organized to serve the needs of their members, whereas other commercial firms are organized to earn profits and returns on invested capital. The co-op's primary purpose is thus to help its members realize higher incomes, lower costs, or more efficient and dependable service.

American cooperatives have traditionally been most successful among the large- and middle-sized farmers who have had the land, capital, and entrepreneurial resources necessary to establish successful businesses. Poor people have benefited little from cooperatives until quite recently.

The most significant attempt prior to the 1960s to establish co-ops among blacks and poor whites on a widespread basis occurred during the New Deal period. The Farm Security Administration, created in 1935, operated a special series of programs designed to help small low-income farmers and was responsible for the formation of 25,543 poor peoples' cooperatives (Baldwin, 1968, pp. 204–07).

Opposition from the agricultural establishment (the USDA extension service, state extension services, state land grant agricultural colleges, county agents, private farm machinery and supply companies, large southern corporations, established cooperatives, and especially the American Farm Bureau Federation), which considered the New Deal antipoverty programs a threat to their economic and political power base, caused this program to incur congressional disapproval, resulting in a series of restrictions beginning in 1943 that seriously limited the Farm Security Administration's ability to continue some of its most important services to the co-ops. In 1946, the Farm Security Administration was discontinued, and a new agency, the Farmers Home Administration, was created in its place.

The rate of failure among Farm Security Administration's co-ops increased slightly between 1943 and 1946, but by the end of June 1946, a total of 84 percent of the 25,543 cooperatives which had been established with funds were still in operation, and more than half (65 percent) of the loans had been completely repaid. Some of these co-ops became strong, viable enterprises. Although some of the Farm Security Administration's co-ops, particularly the smaller and more informal ones, had a rather high incidence of failure because of insufficient volume, poor patronage, and inexperienced management, the rate of failure among these co-ops prior to 1940 was no greater than the bankruptcy rate among private manufacturing enterprises.

The Poor Peoples' Cooperatives*

The present poor peoples' cooperative movement originated during the social ferment of the 1960s. The rapid growth of cooperatives among blacks in the rural South during these years was an outgrowth of civil rights and antipoverty activities. However, cooperatives also were established among poor whites in the South and other areas and Mexican Americans and Indians in the Southwest.

---

* This section is based on Marshall and Godwin, 1971.

Various government agencies helped the co-ops, especially the Office of Economic Opportunity and the Economic Development Administration. The latter has provided grants to cooperatives under its technical assistance program for such purposes as helping economic development programs in rural areas and facilitating the development of marginal enterprises. The former has been the main source of financial assistance to the new organizations. Under the Economic Opportunity Act of 1964, the Farmers Home Administration administered a low-interest (4.125 percent) loan program to help limited-resource co-ops.

Established cooperatives gave very little assistance to the new poor peoples' organizations. Many established organizations were controlled mainly by whites who did not welcome poor blacks as members. In addition, leaders of the established cooperatives did not believe that these poor farmers had the land, capital, or ability to sustain economically viable cooperatives. The established cooperatives also tended to be integral parts of the establishment which had controlled U.S. agricultural policy. They therefore were concerned about the political and social challenge from the poor peoples' organizations.

The origin of what may be called a "movement" among poor peoples' cooperatives in the rural South came in the summer of 1966, when several co-op leaders and members met with representatives of the Southern Regional Council, the Cooperative League, the Office of Economic Opportunity, the National Sharecroppers Fund, the Credit Unions National Association, and other groups at the Mount Beulah Conference Center near Edwards, Mississippi, to exchange ideas and experiences concerning cooperatives for the rural poor. A special continuation committee was appointed to develop a proposal for a cooperative demonstration project, solicit the funds necessary to put it into operation, and make plans for the formation of a federation of poor peoples' cooperatives. As a result of these activities, in June 1967, the Ford Foundation funded the Southern Cooperative Development Program through the Southern Consumers Education Foundation, formed in 1961 by Father A. J. McKnight, a black Catholic priest working in rural Louisiana.

The Federation of Southern Cooperatives

In February 1967, representatives from 22 low-income cooperatives, most of which were affiliated with the Southern Cooperative Development Program, met in Atlanta and established the Federation of Southern Cooperatives. This federation has helped establish new co-ops, has given technical assistance and financial aid to those already established, and generally acts as a "voice" for the rural poor in the South.

After trying unsuccessfully to obtain financial assistance from regular cooperative and commercial lending institutions, the federation instigated the Southern Cooperative Development Fund in August 1969 to provide credit to low-income co-ops and other community-controlled development organizations in the South. Its capital stock is held by cooperatives and outside investors.

Several different types of poor peoples' cooperatives were formed in every area of the county during the 1960s. These include organizations (1) to purchase supplies for farm or household use, (2) to market vegetables, livestock, and other farm products, (3) to purchase machinery, (4) to produce and market handicrafts and garments, (5) to provide a source of credit and to hold savings, (6) to buy land, (7) to catch, grow, and market fish, (8) to provide housing, and (9) to promote general economic development. In 1973 there were more than a hundred of these cooperatives representing over 25,000 poor people in the South, most of whom were black. Other rural cooperatives have been formed among poor people outside the South, especially in California, Appalachia, and the Midwest, but these are not as organized regionally as those in the South.

Appraisal

An analysis of the poor peoples' cooperatives makes it clear that they are not likely to have too significant an impact unless they either gain considerable strength or stimulate reforms to overcome some of the deeply entrenched causes of rural poverty. Really significant changes in the conditions of the poor will depend on developments in agricultural policy; economic development; manpower programs; education, health, and welfare; and measures to combat racial discrimination in employment and other matters affecting human resource development. Cooperatives can influence action for effective policies, but they probably cannot have much impact on the problems of rural poverty unless they produce changes in these areas. A review of the activities of these cooperatives suggests that they can improve their members' income and stimulate their participation in rural communities, especially political affairs, but are not likely to have a significant total developmental impact on rural areas unless they acquire much larger sources of funds than they have had.

During 1970–72, Abt Associates, Inc., in *A Study of Rural Coopera-tives* (1973), evaluated a sample of eighteen low-income rural coopera-tives with the following characteristics:

Product	*Number*
Vegetables	8
Livestock	4
Crafts	6
TOTAL	18

Region	
Appalachia	3
South	8
Midwest	2
Southwest and West	5
TOTAL	18

Racial or Ethnic Composition	
Black	7
Chicano	3
Indian	2
White	4
Mixed:	
Black-white	1
Indian-white	1
TOTAL	18

Its evaluation reached the following conclusions:

(1) Before joining the co-ops, the members' average income from all sources was about $4,000 a year. The average product in-come (difference between value of products sold and the cost of producing them) was $962, an increase of more than 20 per-cent. Using this as a standard against which to compare the average annual growth of rural incomes over a twenty-year period, eleven of the eighteen individual co-ops could be con-sidered successful.

(2) About a third of the members had learned production skills from co-op training and assistance.

(3) Almost three-fourths (73 percent) had not previously produced the co-op product.

(4) In the ten co-ops expressing the goal of increasing membership participation in community affairs, 48 percent of the members reported increased community participation since joining.

(5) The cooperatives had done less than community development corporations (to be discussed later) to reduce outmigration because a smaller percentage of members (10 percent) indicated that they would be living in another area if they had not joined the co-op; in the lowest community development corporations group, 28 percent said they would be living elsewhere.

Abt Associates concluded, on the basis of its evaluation, that cooperatives had demonstrated an ability to achieve institutional viability and had made it clear that "the cooperative can strongly leverage program funds to provide supplementary income gains" (Abt Associates, Inc., *Study*, p. 8). However, some attention was also given to the overall objective of

> . . . promoting economic development and expanding rural economic enterprise. The findings suggest that cooperatives can contribute to such policy objectives, but they do not show the co-op as the central element of a development strategy. While some of the sample cooperatives aspire to be development planning or investment institutions, none have yet implemented such a role. The co-op's economic impact on the community differs little from other export businesses of equivalent sales volume and that volume is comparatively small, even for non-industrialized areas (p. 9).

Rural low-income cooperatives have been extremely fragile organizations, mainly because they are made up mostly of small farmers who are having great difficulty maintaining their competitive positions. While many people who are being displaced from agriculture can and should find better income-producing opportunities in nonfarm jobs, many others might, with appropriate public policies, be able to earn adequate incomes in agriculture or in a combination of farm and rural nonfarm jobs. For example, agricultural reforms which subsidized labor, instead of land and capital, could change the prospects for small farmers and their organizations.

Similarly, an income maintenance system would in effect be a labor subsidy and probably would strengthen co-ops by providing an income base upon which poor farmers could build and by giving them a measure of economic, and hence political, independence. The lower cost of living in rural areas might halt outmigration, particularly for older farmers with limited education. On the other hand, guaranteed incomes and better rural-urban manpower linkages might accelerate the outmigration of younger, better educated people.

In the absence of these kinds of reforms, however, the prospects for poor farmers and their cooperatives are not very bright. Without supportive public policies, co-ops will be able to do little more than fight a delaying action to ease the economic burdens of those who cannot find rural and urban nonfarm jobs.

On the other hand, it is possible to conceive of circumstances in which the co-ops could become a voice for many of the rural poor and, joining with urban friends, produce some significant changes in those institutions responsible for rural poverty. Cooperatives, for example, could join with unions, civil rights groups, and interested foundations in providing a voice for small farmers and the rural poor in the formulation of public policy that could help revitalize rural areas. In the absence of such representation, agricultural and rural development policies will continue to be made by, and reflect the interests of, the most affluent farmers and their political allies.

In order to survive and maintain internal cohesion, a co-op clearly must meet the needs of members or potential members more effectively than the alternatives available to them. The cooperatives also should be based upon careful planning. Economic analyses should be undertaken of all costs, potential commitments, the extent of competition or alternative ways of accomplishing the stated objectives, opposition to be expected from various interest groups, available markets, suitable equipment needs, and the availability of leadership.

Few of the new cooperative enterprises have been preceded by careful planning and economic analysis. To some extent, this was because the co-ops often were formed in desperation to help people in difficult circumstances. However, lack of planning has caused some of the co-ops to suffer serious losses which hamper their subsequent operations.

Role of Management

Successful cooperatives, like other businesses, must have effective management. This requires competent and dedicated administrators.

Moreover, because they must rely heavily on membership patronage, healthy co-ops must adopt a structure which permits active membership participation and control, usually through boards of directors. In addition, the special economic, political, psychological, and social benefits to be derived from co-ops require effective interaction between members, boards of directors, and managers.

The poor peoples' cooperatives formed during the 1960s fall far short of these requirements. The founders of the co-ops often were good organizers but poor administrators, and the recruitment of managers from the membership has been complicated by the members' low educational levels and lack of business experience. In addition, blacks with managerial training and experience are in short supply and usually find better employment opportunities in urban areas.

Virtually all of the low-income co-ops have had record-keeping difficulties. Many members, even those who are on the boards of directors, do not understand their co-op's financial statements or are afraid to question managers about financial matters. Few of the cooperatives had regular bookkeepers; some kept no records at all. However, the Federation of Southern Cooperatives has helped most of its member co-ops overcome some of their accounting difficulties.

Marketing

Most low-income cooperatives have been plagued by marketing problems because of the lack of marketing information and experience. Very few of the leaders, managers, and other personnel know much about such dynamics of marketing as how to make credit checks on brokers in distant locations and other "tricks of the trade." It has been difficult for the leaders of the low-income co-ops to develop the formal and informal contacts that are so essential to success. All businesses suffer from these problems, but for marginal enterprises, the impact can be crucial.

Marketing problems also stem from the inability of some of the agricultural co-ops to obtain sufficient volume to compete with private processors. This is a major problem for them because bargaining power in selling is proportional to the ability to control a supply of uniformly high quality, which is difficult for many small farmers. Marketing experts are therefore needed to work with the farmers to help them produce the correct varieties. The co-ops also need specialists to locate and develop markets for their products.

Membership participation in the form of active use of the cooperatives' services has not been as great as it must be if they are to survive and become economically viable. Membership participation, especially in those whose members are extremely poor, has been limited by harassment from local political and economic leaders who have threatened or bribed potential co-op members. Some poor black farmers, especially those who have worked on plantations for most of their lives, have serious doubts about their ability to succeed in business activities. These skeptics view the struggling co-ops as simply another step in the long line of panaceas which have come and gone without changing their material well-being. It will take sustained and demonstrated success to overcome these attitudes.

But perhaps the main reason many low-income farmers have not patronized the co-ops is that they have not seen any economic advantage in doing so. Some of the cooperatives are so financially weak that they have been unable to pay farmers for produce upon delivery or render the kinds of services (advance payments, and so forth) available from private traders or consumer outlets. People with very low incomes cannot be expected to make economic sacrifices in order to keep the co-ops alive. Cooperatives that are not economically viable must be subsidized, but it is unlikely that the very poor can provide the necessary support.

The agricultural co-ops have also had marketing difficulties because of quality control problems caused by improper grading procedures and inadequate or insufficient processing equipment and storage facilities. This is due in part to the undercapitalization and management problems discussed previously.

Inferior quality produce also has resulted from improper farming practices, but this probably is not as important as the marketing problems. Many of the co-op members are learning to produce crops they have never grown before, and they have not yet mastered the most efficient cultivation methods. Failure to use good seed or fertilizer, to keep crops dry and clean until delivered, or to plant and harvest on time are good examples of this. The co-ops have found it extremely difficult to refuse substandard produce for fear that this would alienate members.

Organizations like the National Sharecroppers Fund and the Federation of Southern Cooperatives are attempting to fill the gap left by the federal government's failure to adopt and implement programs to help poor farmers, but their resources, staff, and experiences are too limited to do the job that needs to be done for all low-income farmers.

Indeed it is difficult to see how the job will be done adequately without a fundamental revision in the federal agricultural and welfare policies.

Cooperatives and Noneconomic Objectives

Although cooperatives are mainly economic organizations, they also have formed the basis for movements to improve the social positions of groups of people and even nations, a role for which they are ideally suited because of their democratic structure and patron-oriented motivation. However, although a co-op often has social and political objectives, these objectives cannot be achieved unless financial problems are resolved.

Established American farm cooperatives have been primarily economic organizations which have relied primarily on "supply management" in order to control markets and protect farm incomes. They consequently take a very dim view of combining economic and social objectives, because the latter might weaken the co-op economically. Poor farmers have not been welcomed as members because they are economically weak. Clearly, though, cooperatives which cater only to immediate economic needs will be less useful to poor people than organizations concerned with a wide range of political and social as well as economic problems.

Many cooperatives have been able to survive because of the cohesiveness they derive from racial, religious, social, or political objectives. The best examples of religious cohesion probably are afforded by the strength of cooperative undertakings in Israel. In the United States, the co-ops in the South have been unified by civil rights objectives. There can be little doubt, for example, that some of them have prospered because blacks have boycotted white establishments for civil rights reasons. Racial unity can cause co-ops to be viable when they do not produce obvious economic advantages, although it is doubtful that racial unity can compensate for clear economic disadvantages for very long if the farmers are extremely poor. Clearly, it would also be advantageous to build organizations for all people similarly situated, regardless of race. This has been difficult to do because white racists have ostracized poor whites who join racially integrated organizations and because black racists sometimes have made it difficult for whites to work with the predominantly black cooperatives. However, in a few cases, especially in the Piedmont area, racially integrated organizations have been formed.

Credit Supply

Even if co-ops are based on felt needs, adopt the proper organizational forms, and attract competent managers and technical assistance, they — like other business enterprises — still need sources of credit to cover emergencies and to permit taking advantage of income-earning opportunities. Credit sources are particularly important for the purchase of land by small farmers. Ideally co-ops should raise at least half of their funds from their members to avoid a heavy debt structure and to give members a stake in the enterprise. Actually, however, the members of the new poor peoples' cooperatives have provided only a small proportion of their capital needs. The very low incomes and assets of the people involved have necessitated this limited membership investment (United Nations, 1954, p. 37). Nevertheless, it probably would be much better for the cooperatives if their members were required to make sacrificial investment in them.

Also, a supervised credit approach, either for loans by the co-ops to their members or by government or other lending institutions to co-ops, probably would facilitate their survival, at least in the initial stages. Excessive reliance on grants could be dangerous because grants do not necessitate the kind of economic discipline required to repay loans. Grants could also produce long-term problems because the co-ops might be unable to sustain the services initially made possible by the grants. A balance clearly needs to be struck between loans and grants to the poor peoples' cooperatives. It would seem to be good practice to have loans for the purchase of tangibles (land, equipment) and grants for intangibles (professional services, educational activities).

Because they have so many managerial and financial difficulties, the low-income co-ops have had great difficulty securing credit from traditional sources. Private institutions naturally try to maximize their profits and minimize their risks and can therefore find better investments than provided by the struggling cooperatives and their members. Most commercial banks refuse to make loans to cooperatives, partly because such loans are risky but also because the banks oppose the idea of low-income cooperatives.

Even those federal credit programs established for people who cannot get credit from other sources often have not been willing to help low-income co-ops. The Banks for Cooperatives, initiated by the federal government in 1933 because established cooperatives were having trouble obtaining credit from traditional sources, have benefited wealthier co-ops by supplying technical services as well as credit. But the Banks for Cooperatives will provide only 50 percent of the funds for any loan application, and even this must be secured by collateral. The Banks for

Cooperatives, like many other federal agencies, are thus more useful to affluent farmers than to co-ops made up of poorer farmers.

The USDA program which has done the most for poor peoples' cooperatives is the equal opportunity loan program created in 1964 and administered by the Farmers Home Administration. Loans from this program have played a major role in supporting the new poor peoples' co-ops, and some administration representatives have been very helpful to poor farmers. We have noted, however, that the administration makes loans to the most affluent of the rural poor, has limited resources, and is vulnerable to political pressures, and in many areas this agency is administered by people who apparently are not always sympathetic to the growth of the poor peoples' cooperatives. Moreover, neither the Office of Economic Opportunity nor the Farmers Home Administration has relied on the supervised credit approach which would coordinate credit and technical assistance.

The timing of both credit and technical assistance is crucial. Most of the current governmental procedures are too cumbersome, involve delays which greatly limit the effectiveness of funds, and are based on invalid rationales or economic theories. Profit maximization theories are adequately suited for private banks, but not for development organizations.

The creation of a federal rural development bank, which would use the "supervised credit" approach, might therefore do much to promote economic development in rural areas. Because such an organization probably would have limited resources, it should help its cooperative borrowers acquire as much leverage as possible through revolving funds, loan guarantees, and pooling arrangements. The rural development bank should be in a position to minimize risks from marginal activities, encourage businesslike enterprises, and provide broad technical assistance. The bank might be financed in much the same way as the original farm credit system, which permitted member organizations to retire federal stock. It could make loans to a wide variety of agencies and individuals engaged in job creation and might have one branch for low-income urban enterprises and another for marginal rural undertakings.

Prospects for the Future

The prospects for poor peoples' cooperatives are not at all clear at this point. A few successful co-ops could become centers of additional activities or could at least stimulate the kinds of programs needed to permit people to make an adequate living and to gain a measure of freedom. If most of the present undertakings can be strengthened sufficiently to permit cooperatives to succeed, their efforts might have a multiplier effect because they could stimulate action by public and private agencies to help the poor while promoting the formation of new co-ops.

But a number of objections have been raised to cooperatives. Their economic feasibility is questioned by those who argue that it will not be possible to provide adequate economic opportunities for poor people. In this view, small farmers are not likely to be able to compete with larger mechanized farms. Blacks and other minorities are at a particular disadvantage, according to these critics, because they own very little land, are uneducated, lack managerial experience, and have inadequate financial resources. Moreover, in this view, the solution to rural or ghetto poverty is not to keep people on the farm or in the ghetto but to increase their productivity and shift them into good nonagricultural jobs.

There is of course no assurance that the poor peoples' cooperatives will become economically viable, although there is little question that they could be. Moreover, as noted in chapter 2, it is not at all clear that small farmers lack economic viability if their credit, marketing, and technical assistance problems could be solved and adequate nonfarm opportunities could be assured. However, few would argue that co-ops alone are permanent solutions to the problems of the rural poor. Many other specific programs are necessary to really improve their conditions. It is our contention that co-ops are simply one approach which can help poor people and small entrepreneurs increase their productivity and incomes.

Nor are the co-ops designed to keep people down on the farm or in the ghetto. They are based on the belief that many people, especially those who are older and poorly educated, will work in marginal enterprises wherever they go and that even some who could make higher incomes in cities will prefer to remain in rural areas and combine farming with nonfarm work. The co-ops therefore are designed to increase the options available to the poor, either in farming and small enterprises or as consumers.

Marginal economic enterprises like cooperatives are criticized because they operate on a scale which is likely to seem insignificant to those accustomed to dealing with more profitable organizations. A net annual increase in incomes of from $300 to $500 for each family — which is estimated to be the net gain from the Farmers Home Administration's economic opportunity loan program or the $962 average product income that Abt Associates, Inc., found in their sample — might cause these enterprises to be considered failures by those accustomed to urban standards. However, for people who average $4,000 and whose incomes are often as low as $800 a year, an increase of $300 to $962 can be very significant. In many rural areas, people who earned $3,000 a year in 1970 were relatively well off.

In order to become economically viable in the long run, cooperatives must also be productive and efficient enough to compete with private firms. This means that their economic operations must be based on the latest technology or must be in activities which are labor intensive and not subject to mechanization. But in the long run, the areas protected from mechanization and agribusiness apparently will be very limited indeed. Therefore in many areas co-ops must be able to acquire the necessary financial resources to obtain equipment that would enable their members to become more productive, to diversify, and therefore to compete with agribusinesses. If small farmers adapt to modern technology, it will have to be through some such organizational form as a cooperative. Moreover, community development co-ops can address themselves to a wide range of problems of the rural and urban poor and at least become organizations through which the poor can influence policy formulation and program implementation.

Although most of the examples we have used have been of agricultural activities, community development corporations can also promote nonfarm economic opportunities. Some cooperatives have stimulated such nonfarm jobs, often in enterprises closely related to their agricultural activities. Such nonfarm activities as the manufacturing of fertilizer and of farm supplies have been of utmost importance to cooperatives among more affluent groups but have limited success among the newer low-income cooperatives. As noted in chapter 2, however, the newer cooperatives could play a role in implementing the Rural Development Act of 1972. Moreover, cooperatives have been formed among small nonfarm enterprises to strengthen their marketing and purchasing activities.

Nonfarm economic opportunities are important to small farmers and their families because few small farmers receive most of their income from farming alone. In undertaking farm and nonfarm as well as economic and social activities, cooperatives resemble community development corporations.

COMMUNITY DEVELOPMENT CORPORATIONS

The community development corporations are considered by some observers to have considerable promise for rural development. They are locally controlled, tax-exempt organizations with a wide range of human resource objectives. They attempt to do such things as increase jobs and income, provide better housing, improve the services available from governments to poor or minority communities, and provide needed social services not available from government. Thus this kind of entity commends itself as a rural development agency because it addresses itself to many of the diverse needs of rural people (see Twentieth Century Fund, 1971).

Perhaps some concrete examples will illustrate the nature of these corporations. One such organization is the six thousand-member Southeast Alabama Self-Help Association, operating in twelve black counties in Alabama. This association, organized in 1965 and chartered in 1967, grew out of a community education program conducted by Tuskegee Institute. It is governed by a board of directors with representatives from each of the counties in which it operates. Its initial purpose was to provide aid to poor people by: (1) obtaining social services from unresponsive (and often hostile) local agencies, (2) helping poor blacks retain their land, and (3) helping local residents build better water systems.

With the help of funding of $480,000 from the Office of Economic Opportunity in 1968, the association became a rural economic development corporation. In addition to these funds, it has received $575,000 from the Ford Foundation (*Community Development Corporation*, 1973). Among other things, this association has helped local small businesses, operated a credit union, organized a feeder-pig cooperative, and undertaken housing and industrial development activities.

Another rural community development corporation is Mississippi Action for Community Education, organized in the Mississippi Delta in 1965 as the basis of a merger of several self-help groups with a constituency of some twenty thousand people. Its initial objective was to provide training for community organizers, the development of adult basic education programs, and activities to improve the delivery of social services by local government agencies. But it gave greater emphasis to economic and business development during the late 1960s and early 1970s.

The Delta Foundation, with which the Mississippi program is affiliated, provides venture capital to a variety of black-owned businesses, including a blue jeans factory, a metal stamping plant, and a chain of community-owned "superettes" with a thousand stockholders and gross sales of about $1,500,000. The Mississippi Action for Community Education program has also responded to grossly inadequate health facilities in the Mississippi Delta by organizing mobile health units, training paramedical personnel, and recruiting medical doctors.

Federal support for community development corporations was authorized by a 1966 amendment to Title I of the Economic Opportunity Act of 1964 and administered by the Labor Department, the Economic Development Act, the Office of Economic Opportunity, and the Farmers Home Administration. In fiscal year 1969, the Office of Economic Opportunity assumed full responsibility for the program. Abt Associates, Inc., evaluated thirty Office of Economic Opportunity-funded urban and rural community development corporations which had generated 2,066 direct permanent jobs and 5,455 temporary jobs in 250 business and other activities. The total annual wage bill of these community development corporations was $10.2 million, representing an increase of $1.7 million in annual wages over wages received by these employees before they went to work for the community development corporations. Rural corporations had heavy concentrations of manufacturing employment in their ventures, while urban organizations showed more balance between manufacturing, retail, and service activities.

The community development corporations evaluated by Abt Associates, Inc., reported a low $82 average annual wage increase for nonmanagerial personnel. There were even a substantial number of cases where community development corporation employees were paid less on an annual basis than they had been on noncorporation jobs, in part because a sizable proportion of corporation employees worked part time. Salary gains were lowest in the highly competitive retail and wholesale trade sectors, while workers in the construction sector experienced substantial improvements. Almost half of the corporation employees (48 percent) previously were unemployed or underemployed.

The Abt Associates, Inc., evaluation came to the following conclusions on critical issues:

(1) The program, ". . . given all of the sources of funding made available to date, will probably not achieve an appreciable impact on the unemployment problems in any of the 30 sites evaluated" (*Evaluation*, 1973, p. 13). Based on the average cost of creating a job of $6,200 in urban and $8,000 in rural areas, Abt Associates, Inc., estimate it would take forty years to close the unemployment gap between areas where the community development corporations operated and surrounding

areas. The report also found that corporations in large urban areas had been more adequately funded than those in smaller urban and rural areas.

(2) Job creation costs of these corporations have been highest in manufacturing and lowest in construction, and financial performance was strongly influenced by the previous experience of managers. "Ventures which have hired and trained inexperienced managers have not performed as well financially as those which have hired experienced managers" (Abt Associates, Inc., *Evaluation*, p. 16). The ventures seem to have performed better when the corporation shared ownership with the managers of their ventures.

(3) "Program benefits could be increased substantially if a greater proportion of private to federal funds could be achieved" (*Evaluation*, p. 20). Abt Associates, Inc., thought more private funds could be attracted to the corporations if private interests had greater participation on advisory boards.

(4) The community development corporations could have greater impact, according to the report, if funding were increased for venture capital and administration and if stronger links were established between corporations and local resources.

The community development corporations are taking an approach that seeks to deal with the social and economic problems of the rural poor. A crucial determinant of their success would appear to be their ability to attract funds and competent administrative staffs. The Ford Foundation has decided to make substantial investments of its funds in these organizations, but really significant resources must come from federal and private financial sources if the corporations are to make any impact on rural social and economic problems. Nevertheless, this model is sufficiently promising to warrant careful attention, with a view to identifying activities — like construction — that seem to have the highest payoff per dollar of investment. Such corporations can also be combined with cooperatives, as was the case with the Southeast Alabama Self-Help Association. Indeed, as noted earlier, many of the cooperatives' activities closely resemble those of community corporations in concentrating on social and economic activities.

COLLECTIVE BARGAINING IN AGRICULTURE

Primarily because of the successes of Cesar Chavez and the United Farm Workers in California and Florida in the 1960s and early 1970s, collective bargaining by agricultural workers has stimulated the apprehensions of growers and the hopes of many agricultural workers and their sympathizers. The growers are afraid that collective bargaining will bring economic ruin to farmers, and the agricultural workers and their supporters hope collective bargaining will raise their wages and working conditions to the level of unionized workers in other sectors. Both sides are appealing to the public for support. A number of farm industrial relations bills have been introduced in Congress, and a number of states have passed or are considering measures to regulate agricultural industrial relations.

This section explores the present status of collective bargaining in agriculture, discusses some of the factors influencing collective bargaining in this sector, and presents some conclusions concerning the desirability and prospects for collective bargaining among farm workers.

Status of Collective Bargaining in Agriculture

Although there had been a long history of efforts to establish collective bargaining in agriculture before World War II, these efforts were largely unsuccessful. Following World War II, a number of attempts were made to organize agricultural workers, especially in California, Texas, Louisiana, Florida, and some midwestern states. In 1947, the AFL chartered the National Agricultural Workers Union with H. L. Mitchell, a founder of the Southern Tenant Farmers Union, as its president. Also in 1947, this union launched an organizing drive among the workers at the giant Di Georgio grape fields in California. However, Di Georgio was able to defeat the strike through the importation of strikebreakers and a federal injunction against picketing.

Another unsuccessful strike began in Starr County, Texas, in 1966. This strike was undertaken by the Independent Workers Association against three large melon growers in that county of the Rio Grande valley on the Mexican border. The growers responded with a temporary restraining order prohibiting pickets at the struck farms. Ironically, the injunction was issued under a Texas law prohibiting "secondary picketing" which had been ruled unconstitutional by the Texas Supreme Court seven years earlier and was ruled unconstitutional by a three-judge federal district court in July 1972 (MEDRANO VS ALLEE). Although the injunction undoubtedly hurt the union, the importation of strikebreakers and the use of Texas Rangers against strikers and their sympathizers also contributed to the defeat of this strike.

The main successful agricultural workers' organizing campaign began with the grape strike by Chavez and the United Farm Workers around Delano, California, in 1965. Despite the growers' use of all the familiar anti-union tactics, this effort succeeded after a long and difficult strike for a number of reasons, including:

(1) Grape workers are more highly skilled and therefore more difficult to replace than other agricultural workers.

(2) Grape workers were more highly concentrated geographically than other agricultural workers.

(3) The termination of the bracero law in 1964 closed this source of strikebreakers.

(4) The labor movement gave the United Farm Workers considerable support.

(5) Cesar Chavez was able to evoke public sympathy with the strike, causing a nationwide grape boycott to be relatively successful.

Schenley was the first company to sign with the union, but in the early fall of 1966, following the Schenley settlement in April, Christian Brothers and Novitiate recognized the union. After Di Georgio signed with the United Farm Workers on April 1, 1967, some thirty growers followed suit.

Although the unionization of grape growers was highly significant, it by no means established collective bargaining as an accepted institution in California's agriculture. Grape growers so far represent the only significant unionization, but these workers account for only 1 or 2 percent of the California farm labor force. In Florida, the United Farm Workers succeeded in organizing Coca Cola's food division in February 1972, but apparently encountered as much (or more) resistance from Florida growers as it had in California and Texas. Chavez and his associates are also encountering opposition from the mainly black and Caucasian Florida workers on the grounds that chicanos from the Southwest cannot relate very effectively to the problems of Florida farm workers.

The United Farm Workers launched organizing drives to inculcate laborers in other California crops, especially lettuce, but had meager resources and encountered mounting opposition from the growers and their political allies. The union was particularly concerned about legal threats to the boycott, which probably proved decisive in forcing the grape employers to bargain. Moreover, it faced jurisdictional conflicts with the powerful teamsters union of the AFL-CIO, to which some growers are reported to have turned as a means of keeping Chavez out.

The teamsters agreed in March 1971 to give up their contracts if the employers were willing, but this agreement was of limited value to the farm workers — because the lettuce growers do not seem to be too eager to sign with the United Farm Workers, especially where the union seeks to establish hiring halls.

In December 1972, the California Supreme Court dissolved injunctions against the United Farm Workers, which had been filed under a California law against jurisdictional disputes, on the grounds that the employers had selected the teamsters union and there was no evidence that the workers wanted that union to represent them. In January 1973, the United Farm Workers brought suit against 160 agribusinesses and the teamsters union in federal district court, claiming a conspiracy by the teamsters and employers against the United Farm Workers. The United Farm Workers also charged racial bias by the teamsters and the growers (New York *Times*, January 5, 1973).

The most serious threat to the United Farm Workers came during the summer of 1973, when the teamsters started signing contracts with the grape growers who had previously signed with the United Farm Workers. The main complaint expressed by the growers was the hiring hall, which gave the farm workers control over referrals. The farm workers insisted on the hiring hall as a means of distributing work equitably. The conflict became a national issue when George Meany, president of the AFL-CIO, met with Frank Fitzsimmons, president of the International Brotherhood of Teamsters (which was expelled from the AFL-CIO in 1957 because of corrupt influences in the teamsters).

Chavez had walked out of peace talks with West Coast teamster leader Einer Mohn on August 9, 1973, to protest the International Brotherhood of Teamsters having signed agreements with thirty more growers after the talks began. The day after Chavez walked out of the negotiations, Fitzsimmons wrote to the thirty growers, repudiating the agreements and denouncing the International Brotherhood of Teamsters' field representatives for signing the agreements while talks with Chavez were going on.

However, Fitzsimmons' letter did not settle the matter, because Chavez announced that he did not believe the contracts had in fact been invalidated. Moreover, contracts signed before August 9, 1973, between the growers and the teamsters in other crops and in grapes remained in effect. The United Farm Workers therefore struck the grape growers and resumed its nationwide consumer boycott. Chavez halted picketing in the Delano area after two farm workers were killed in picket line violence (Jenkins, 1973). In September 1973, negotiations in Washington between Chavez, Fitzsimmons, and President George Meany of the AFL-CIO led to an agreement that the United Farm Workers would have jurisdiction over field workers and the teamsters over those in the sheds.

In conclusion, then, it seems accurate to describe the present condition of collective bargaining in agriculture as one where the unions have established small and isolated beachheads but where their enemies have launched full-scale counterattacks.

Prospects for Agricultural Unionization

We can judge the prospects for agricultural unionism by considering the extent to which the following traditional impediments to agricultural unionism still prevail. First, because the ability to bring economic pressure to bear against employers is a basic determinant for private sector collective bargaining, the most serious impediment to organizing agricultural workers probably has been the large supply of potential strikebreakers available. In the South, these strikebreakers are usually low-paid, unemployed, and underemployed sharecroppers and other agricultural workers whose ranks have increased greatly in the post-World War II period by more than 2.5 million workers displaced because of technological change and U.S. agricultural policy. In addition, labor surpluses in the Southwest have been augmented by the importation of workers from Mexico.

Second, seasonality of work and the migrant status of many farm workers do not tend to induce interest in and attachment to a permanent union. In 1970 only 22 percent of the hired farm work force listed farm labor as their chief occupation. About 56 percent (primarily housewives and students) were not in the labor force for the majority of the year. Domestic migratory workers composed about 8 percent of the total hired work force.

Third, workers are highly scattered, only a few to a farm. In 1964 farms without hired labor or with little hired labor constituted 88 percent of all farms and accounted for 50 percent of all farm products sold. However, 21 percent of the largest farms (those with sales of $100,000 or more) had more than fifteen man-years of hired labor. It is estimated that application of the jurisdictional rule applied by the National Labor Relations Board to some agricultural processing operations — $50,000 in interstate commerce — would cover only 3.5 percent of farms but 45 percent of the farm labor force.

Fourth, organizing costs are high, especially without National Labor Relations Act or similar coverage. Since most farm workers have low incomes, if farm labor continues to be excluded from statutory coverage, union efforts to obtain recognition as their bargaining agents and to obtain agreements will have to depend upon force or pressure, pickets, and boycotts, which are expensive and uncertain.

And finally, agricultural workers are excluded from National Labor Relations Act coverage. While such coverage may not be a major factor in union growth, it is not without significance. As noted above, the lack of this coverage has caused organizing to be more expensive. In addition, the coverage applies a moral sanction to collective bargaining that influences public opinion and worker attitudes about bargaining. Indeed, the absence of such coverage has even caused some observers to believe that collective bargaining in agriculture is "illegal" and "wrong."

Despite these obstacles to union growth, several trends appear to improve the chances of organizing farm workers. First is the growing size and vertical integration of agricultural industries. Vertical integration encourages unionization by making work forces larger and often increases the agricultural workers' attachment to a particular firm. Moreover, vertical integration increases the nonagricultural labor movement's interest in unionizing agricultural workers in order to gain control throughout the production process. The significance of this point was dramatized for unions in California when employers transferred some operations from unionized packing sheds to nonunion field workers.

In the nonagricultural sector, there is a strong correlation between farm size and union strength, probably because large firms are prime organizing targets and because the workers in these firms are more favorably disposed toward organization than are the employees of small firms where communication is easier and there are closer employer-employee relations. Vertical integration also probably will cause public opinion to be more favorably disposed toward collective bargaining than it was toward the unionization of small family farms.

Second, there is increasing union and public support. The AFL-CIO, its constituents, and other independent unions are now supporting farm workers' unions both actively and financially. In addition, churches, civil rights organizations, minority groups, and students are actively supporting the United Farm Workers. The media also appear to be lending a sympathetic ear and voice, thus arousing moral support across the nation. A major accomplishment by Chavez and the United

Farm Workers has been to involve the public in the organizing contest. If this supportive interest continues, it may well have a significant impact on breaking down traditional attitudinal barriers to agricultural unionism among hesitant farm workers as well as employers.

A third trend is an increasing support for inclusion of agricultural workers under the National Labor Relations Act. Although the Nixon administration has urged congressional action on this issue, differences of opinion about coverage and administration have tended to keep related bills bottled up in committee.

However, as noted earlier, coverage under the Act will not automatically ensure successful union organization. Success in bargaining, historically, seems to have depended primarily on economic factors influencing a union's ability to compel recalcitrant employers to bargain. Nevertheless, coverage undoubtedly would create a more favorable moral environment to organizing.

And finally there is success of the United Farm Workers' organizing committee. Many farm workers' union advocates and sympathizers point to the accomplishments of the United Farm Workers, suggesting that its success can be imitated by other farm workers' groups. But transferability of success is by no means certain. Several of the factors contributing to the advance of the farm workers will not necessarily be present elsewhere. Grapes require special care for nearly nine months of the year. Thus the labor force is less mobile, more skilled, and better paid than many other agricultural workers. Furthermore, there are more than seventy grape ranches concentrated in the Delano area, requiring a large pool of homogeneous labor. Geographic concentration contributes to unionization by reducing the cost of organizing each worker and providing the union a base from which to extend unionization.

The United Farm Workers' lettuce boycott, by contrast, seems to be more difficult because consumers probably are less willing to forego lettuce, because union lettuce is more difficult to distinguish from non-union lettuce, and because lettuce growing is not as heavily concentrated geographically and does not require relatively skilled workers for as many months of the year. Moreover, the United Farm Workers could lose its hard-won gains even in grapes if it is unable to prevail in its contest with the teamsters.

Public Policy

Mainly because of their political and economic weaknesses, agricultural workers were excluded from coverage under the Wagner Act of

1935. Many observers consider this exclusion to have been detrimental to the unionization of agricultural workers. Opponents of collective bargaining in agriculture initially argued against coverage for these workers on the grounds that agriculture was different from nonagricultural activity in that the perishable nature of farm products made employers vulnerable to strikes at harvest time. However, this argument is rejected by advocates of collective bargaining because the damage done an employer in nonagricultural industries has never been considered a reason to deny National Labor Relations Act coverage. In addition, the labor of agricultural workers also is a "perishable" commodity which cannot be replaced once it is lost. Moreover, those who favor excluding agricultural workers assume that strikes will be completely successful at harvest time — which, in view of the impediments to agricultural unions discussed earlier, is doubtful.

It is also unlikely that the unions would have an interest in ruining employers even if they could. Once collective bargaining is established, union leaders ordinarily are as interested in the economic health of their industries as employers. Collective bargaining has proved to be a very flexible institution, based on compromise of employer and worker interests, and clearly is adaptable to agricultural conditions. Indeed, collective bargaining has a long history of success in the Hawaiian sugar and pineapple industries. If strikes at harvest time are considered to be damaging, the parties could include no-strike clauses in their contracts.

As noted earlier, experience seems to demonstrate that laws actually are not major factors in union growth. Clearly, the absence of coverage under the Act does not prohibit collective bargaining but merely does not provide means to resolve representation questions and regulate unfair labor practices. Collective bargaining, therefore, is based mainly on union and employer ability to inflict economic losses on (or to withhold benefits from) each other. If unions exert enough pressure on employers to gain recognition, they can acquire bargaining rights whether or not they represent a majority of the employer's employees. Since agricultural workers are relatively unskilled, operate in labor surplus areas, and have limited ability to withhold their labor because low incomes force them to work, they have considerable difficulty forcing employers to bargain. The United Farm Workers therefore was forced to resort to consumer and secondary boycotts to gain collective bargaining rights.

The United Farm Workers' organizing activities have caused some significant changes in positions concerning collective bargaining. Although unions generally have regarded National Labor Relations Act coverage as beneficial to union growth, the United Farm Workers does not favor such coverage. Chavez argues that the Act, as amended by the Taft-Hartley and Landrum-Griffin Acts, prohibiting such tactics as secondary boycotts and putting limitations on organizational picketing, would do the union more damage than good. He therefore favors coverage only if the law were more like the original Wagner Act, which prohibited employer unfair labor practices but placed no restrictions on unions. Chavez thinks agricultural unions should have at least twelve years under a Wagner-type statute, as nonagricultural unions did before the Wagner Act was amended by Taft-Hartley in 1947. Because of his support in liberal and labor circles, Chavez' opposition to extending National Labor Relations Act coverage to agriculture has removed a great deal of support from this proposal.

Employers also have had some second thoughts about collective bargaining policy in agriculture because of the success of the United Farm Workers' tactics. Employer groups have been mainly responsible for preventing the adoption of any public policy with respect to collective bargaining in agriculture, but they want protection from strikes and boycotts now that the unions have some prospects of success with these weapons. Growers therefore have succeeded in getting laws passed which regulate agricultural labor relations in Arizona, Idaho, Kansas, Oklahoma, Oregon, and South Dakota. In addition, at least seven bills regulating farm labor relations have been introduced in Congress. Because of California's size and importance, one of the most significant recent public policy developments was the unsuccessful 1972 campaign to pass a California law permitting growers to seek court orders prohibiting agricultural strikes for ninety days. The proposed California law also would have greatly restricted picketing and boycotts. The defeat of this proposal in the November 1972 elections should boost the United Farm Workers' prospects in California.

While National Labor Relations Act coverage would not necessarily stimulate collective bargaining, because unions still would have to strike to gain contracts, it is clearly in the public interest to have some machinery to resolve recognition issues and prevent unfair practices by unions and employers. Such coverage would make secondary boycotts illegal, but primary and informational boycotts could continue. In other words, agricultural unions could not ask other unions to refuse to handle goods or to strike (secondary) employers handling agricultural products, but it would still be legal for farm workers' organizations to persuade consumers to boycott nonunion products. Conflicts over recognition questions often are very bitter, so some machinery to resolve these and prevent some forms of intimidation and coercion by unions and employers would be in the public interest.

Conclusions

The history and current trends among agricultural workers suggest that unionization will expand slowly in this sector. This is true because while many of the traditional impediments to agricultural unionization persist, there is growing public sentiment for collective bargaining. Moreover, the growth in farm size will create an agricultural working class with limited upward occupational mobility, which always has been a precondition for unionization. Some form of collective bargaining legislation for agriculture undoubtedly will be adopted, but it is difficult to say whether the legislation will help or hurt organizing, compared with current activity. A law modeled after the Wagner Act, advocated by the United Farm Workers, probably would stimulate organization. However, even with a Wagner-type law, the spread of collective bargaining still would depend heavily on the union's strength, determination, leadership, and motivation to organize and the ease with which employers could operate during strikes. Moreover, growing farm size, the spread of unionism in nonfarm employment, the reduction of unemployment and underemployment in the rural South, and a reduction in the flow of workers across the Mexican border would strengthen unions in the South and Southwest.

While there is considerable disagreement over the form national policy for collective bargaining in agriculture should take, there are few convincing arguments for differentiating this sector from any other. Farm workers have been excluded from the National Labor Relations Act and other social legislation more because of the political power of employer interests than because of agriculture's unique characteristics. Political weakness is hardly a legitimate reason to deny people equal protection of laws otherwise considered to be in the public interest.

Although the long-run prospects for collective bargaining in agriculture probably are good, unions in this sector probably will have more general influence on public policy than they will on agricultural wages and working conditions. This is true because labor organizations will have difficulty raising the wages of very many agricultural workers through traditional collective bargaining procedures. Since unions must convince their members and potential members that organization brings tangible benefits, unions probably will demonstrate results more through changes in public policy than through collective bargaining.

However, as the numbers of agricultural workers decline, their skills increase, and their work becomes less casual, unions will be more likely to affect wages, hours, and working conditions, particularly if they are able to control the reduced supplies of labor through referral systems. Similarly, rising demand for agricultural products and declining supplies of agricultural labor will strengthen collective bargaining in agriculture.

Collective bargaining by agricultural workers has been impeded by the economics of this sector, by U.S. agricultural policy, and by the absence of an effective rural development policy. Historically, agricultural wages have been low because of low productivity, seasonality, and the highly competitive nature of agriculture. The demand for much agricultural labor has been highly elastic because of the competitiveness of agricultural product markets, the limited skills required, the availability of human and mechanical substitutes, and the high ratio of labor costs to total costs. Unions will have great difficulty raising the wages of agricultural workers as long as these conditions persist.

In view of these economic conditions, if they are to be successful in the long run, unions will not only have to represent the interests of those workers who remain in agriculture, and have higher skills and greater attachment to particular employers, but also must:

(1) Attempt to effect agricultural policies which accelerate the displacement of agricultural labor by subsidizing land and capital

(2) Pay attention to the economic problems of small farmers whose survival influences the size of agricultural work forces and provides alternative sources of income for agricultural workers

(3) Promote measures to limit the supply of workers entering the United States

(4) Attempt to become more influential as labor market institutions controlling jobs and the supplies of casual agricultural labor

(5) Influence manpower and rural development programs to prepare workers for nonfarm jobs and to either attract industry to rural areas to provide additional sources of income for farm workers or help farm workers prepare for and move to nonfarm jobs outside rural areas

(6) Combine farm and nonfarm organizing activities, because, as noted earlier, most agricultural workers and small farmers get most of their income off the farm

UNIONS IN THE RURAL NONFARM SECTOR

With few exceptions, unions in the rural nonfarm sector have been relatively weak but are stronger than those in agriculture. The exceptions are places where unions have been strong in certain large, resource-oriented, capital-intensive industries — such as pulp and paper, where labor is a small part of total costs and workers have been relatively skilled (conditions which give workers considerable bargaining power).

For the most part, however, rural industries have not been very well organized (Marshall, 1967). The main reason for this undoubtedly is the marginal nature of rural industry. Much of this industry is labor intensive, competitive, and low wage. Unions have rarely been successful in such industries, because their competitive nature makes it difficult for unions to achieve tangible economic benefits for their members. These industries also have relatively low skill requirements and often are located in labor surplus areas, both of which limit the unions' power to win strikes and therefore their ability to organize recalcitrant employers. Rural nonfarm workers are also likely to be more difficult to organize because their agrarian backgrounds and value systems do not incline them to organized activity. It is likewise much more expensive for unions to sign up scattered rural workers than it is for them to organize workers concentrated in urban labor markets.

Finally, rural power structures are likely to take strong anti-union positions. In part, this is because agribusiness industries have feared unionization because of the implications of strikes at harvest time and because agriculture has been a highly competitive industry where each employer is afraid unions would give him a competitive disadvantage. But even rural nonfarm business interests are afraid of unions, because they too have been labor-intensive, highly competitive industries.

Local rural community leaders usually have programs to promote industrialization. These industrial development activities usually take on anti-union philosophies because the absence of unions frequently is considered an inducement to the kind of industry likely to be attracted to many rural areas. There was a time when these rural power structures translated their anti-union attitudes into police action and other forms of physical violence against union organizers. Although these more overtly physical forms of resistance are no longer as common, the underlying attitudes remain, to create fear among the workers who might wish to unionize.

References

Abt Associates, Inc. *An Evaluation of the Special Impact Program: Interim Report, 1973.* Vol. I. Cambridge, Massachusetts: Abt Associates, Inc. 1973.

————. *A Study of Rural Cooperatives.* Cambridge, Massachusetts: Abt Associates, Inc. 1973.

Baldwin, Sidney. *Poverty and Politics.* Chapel Hill: University of North Carolina Press. 1968.

Community Development Corporations: A Strategy for Depressed Rural and Urban Areas. Policy Paper. New York: Ford Foundation. 1973.

Jenkins, Evan. "Chavez Calls on Teachers to Back His Farm Union." New York *Times*, August 24, 1973.

Marshall, Ray. *Labor in the South.* Cambridge, Massachusetts: Harvard University Press. 1967.

————; and Godwin, Lamond. *Cooperatives and Rural Poverty in the South.* Baltimore: The Johns Hopkins University Press. 1971.

Medrano vs Allee, 80 LRRM 3016 (1972).

New York *Times*, January 5, 1973.

Twentieth Century Fund Task Force on Community Development Corporations. *New Hope for the Inner City.* A report. New York: Twentieth Century Fund. 1971.

United Nations. *Rural Progress through Cooperatives.* 1954.

6. Wages and Unemployment Insurance

Agricultural workers have been excluded from many forms of protective legislation which nonfarm workers take for granted. Coverage by this legislation has important manpower implications because it affects the willingness of workers to remain in agriculture and the extent to which employers are willing to hire and train workers. In short, these measures have considerable influence on employment and working conditions.

Minimum Wages

In 1966 Congress extended the minimum wage to about 2 percent of the nation's farms, which employed about half of the hired farm work force and two-thirds of the migrants. Coverage was extended only to those farms using five hundred or more man-days of labor (about seven men) in any quarter during the preceding year. The minimum was gradually raised from $1.00 in 1967 to $1.30 beginning February 1, 1969. In addition, nine states had minimum wage coverage for farm workers in 1970, and two additional states — California and Wisconsin — extend coverage to minors and women. However, these state laws generally have restricted coverage which excludes many farm workers.

The impact of the Fair Labor Standards Act coverage was uneven. About 70 percent of the workers affected were on labor-intensive fruit, vegetable, and nut farms. At the time the law became effective, about 45 percent of those concerned made less than a dollar an hour, and about three-fourths of these were in the South. The estimated extent to which the farm wage bill had to be raised to meet these standards was 12 per-

cent in the nation and 20 percent in the South. However, the impact of
the law was minimized by permitting growers to take credit for board
and housing they provided their workers. There was very little evidence
that the legal minimum caused increases in the wages of people not
covered. Between May 1965 and May 1967, the average hourly earnings of hired farm workers rose by $0.28 in the nation and $0.34 in the
South (Coles, 1969, p. 56).

The extension of the federal minimum apparently had little measurable impact on the trend in employment. The decline in farm employment has continued, but the decline was greater on uncovered farms
(31 percent) than on those covered by the law (11 percent). In the
South the rate of decline was about the same for both categories of farms
in the first nine months, while employment actually increased 55 percent
on covered farms and declined 32 percent on uncovered farms in the
West.

The Labor Department studied the impact of the dollar minimum
wage in 52 geographic areas that had at least five thousand man-months
of employment at less than a dollar an hour and found that wages had
risen in nearly every area without having the decline in agricultural employment perceptibly accelerated ("Agricultural Minimum Wage Coverage Impact," May 1968; U.S. Department of Labor, 1969).

It would be a mistake, however, to conclude from this evidence that
the minimum wage has had *no* influence on employment, because it undoubtedly has had, even though the impact is difficult to measure.
Moreover, the impact of the minimum wage might have occurred over a
time period longer than that measured by the Labor Department. The
problem of course is that other factors are at work, including mechanization, the decline in small farms, and the consolidation of large farms into
corporate agricultural supply systems. Moreover, mechanization and
rationalization are influenced by such factors as the ability to control
supplies of agricultural labor; rising nonwage labor costs, such as housing improvements and anticipated unemployment and workmen's compensation coverage; and the fear of unionization.

A number of factors limit the detrimental impact of minimum wages
on employment. The most important of these is the fact that a uniform
minimum wage which raises labor costs across the board can cause price
increases that will not have too much impact on the demand for agricultural products, generally price inelastic. In addition, the minimum
wage requirements of various states and the federal government are
widely violated, sometimes outright and sometimes by various subter-

fuges such as the use of piece rates. Moreover, many farmers pay wages in cash and keep no records, therefore making it difficult to prove their violation of the law. The Migrant Legal Action Program has succeeded in getting back pay awards against growers who have shorted workers on minimum wages (Janson, 1971, p. 1).

The employment effects of minimum wages are also minimized because wages affect the supply of labor as well as the demand. Indeed many agricultural employers now advocate minimum wage coverage and the extension of other protective legislation to agriculture because they realize that improved conditions will help them compete for labor. If higher wages attract more productive workers into agriculture, labor costs need not rise with rising wages. As nonfarm wages, welfare, and other income maintenance payments rise, employers can attract workers only by raising wages. Moreover, in a competitive industry like agriculture, where unions are not strong enough to equalize wages, employers as well as workers benefit from uniform minimum wages.

Collective bargaining would be a better way to fix wages because it would permit joint determination by unions and employers, based on the realities in each situation, but in the absence of unions, minimum wage coverage is a "second best" solution. Therefore although other measures should be taken to minimize the impact of minimum wages, these benefits should be extended to agricultural workers on the same basis as those in nonagricultural activities. Indeed this position was supported by the Senate Committee on Labor and Public Welfare which reported, at the time of the 1966 amendments, that:

> It is the intention of this committee that all workers under the Act be subject to a single minimum wage. The committee action in limiting the pattern of escalation for agriculture at this time to $1.30 in February 1969 is to ensure that there be a careful evaluation of the effects of applying a minimum wage to agriculture. The committee expects that agriculture will adjust without adverse effects as have other industries under the Act and that additional increases will be provided in the future.

Since serious adverse effects have not materialized, it is time to extend equal coverage to all workers.

UNEMPLOYMENT INSURANCE

Repeated attempts to get unemployment compensation coverage for farm workers have failed. Proposals to extend unemployment insurance coverage to farm workers have been included in all recent administration recommendations (Lovell, 1971). The AFL-CIO has testified in favor of this inclusion. The proposals made in connection with the Employment Security Amendments of 1970 would have extended unemployment insurance coverage to all farms with three hundred man-days of hired farm labor in any calendar quarter. This would have extended coverage to 572,000 farm workers on 67,000 farms, or 2 percent of the farms and 40 percent of all farm workers. The Senate Finance Committee would have included this coverage, but the House Ways and Means Committee's bill failed to include it. In conference, the Senate provision was dropped, and the conferees added a provision directing the Secretary of Labor to research the effects of extending coverage to agricultural workers.*

The research done thus far on the effects of unemployment insurance coverage in cases where employers have elected coverage — as some have done in Hawaii, where farm workers have unemployment coverage, and in Puerto Rico, where coverage extends to sugar cane workers — indicated no insurmountable cost or administrative problems. Indeed these problems are not likely to be any greater than those encountered in other seasonal industries, such as construction. According to a 1971 statement by Roger Rossi,** after a review of existing research:

> The findings in these research efforts, in combination with the known changes taking place in agriculture, make continued exclusion of agricultural employment anachronistic. . . . All available evidence indicates that no insurmountable obstacles would arise in providing this needed and long-overdue protection to a farm worker to whom the consequences of involuntary unemployment are at least equal to those of his societal brothers now covered under this program ("The Farm Worker," 1971, p. 21).

WORKMEN'S COMPENSATION

Despite the fact that agriculture is one of the nation's most hazardous occupations, farm workers are largely excluded from workmen's compensation legislation that is compulsory for workers in other industries. Exclusion from this legislation denies the farm worker income during

---

* The author is indebted to Howard D. Samuel, vice president of the Amalgamated Clothing Workers of America and a member of the National Manpower Advisory Committee, for information on the effects of unemployment insurance coverage, the results of efforts to secure passage, and the AFL-CIO's position on the extension of this and other legislation to farm workers.

** Chief of the Division of Program Research with the Office of Actuarial and Research Services, Unemployment Insurance Service, Manpower Administration.

periods of disability, medical services, rehabilitation training and benefits, and death and burial benefits to workers killed on the job. The original argument for excluding farm workers was that this industry was not mechanized and therefore not very hazardous, but this is scarcely true now. Indeed today the fatality rate in agriculture is exceeded only by those in mining and construction (National Safety Council, 1967, p. 23).

Although 22 states and Puerto Rico now extend some kind of workmen's compensation coverage to farm workers, most of these states have provisions restricting coverage of these workers. The only states covering farm workers on the same basis as other workers are California, Hawaii, Massachusetts, New Jersey, Ohio, and Vermont, as does Puerto Rico.

An important recent development was the extension of the Occupational Safety Act of 1970 to farm workers, one of the few times agricultural workers have received equal coverage from protective legislation. This Act, which created an Occupational Safety and Health Appeals Commission whose decisions are subject to review by a U.S. court of appeals, provides for federal enforcement of safety standards. This law requires employers to provide places of employment free of hazards likely to cause workers serious bodily harm. The standards are promulgated by the Secretary of Labor, who may, however, approve state standards if the latter are at least as effective as those issued by the federal government. This law also created a commission to evaluate state workmen's compensation laws.

Although action on extending workmen's compensation to all farm workers perhaps should wait for the results of the new study commission, it is difficult to see why hired farm workers should be exempt from these laws. Experience in the states with this coverage demonstrates the feasibility of equal coverage for farm workers. Moreover, fifteen European countries apparently have had satisfactory experiences with programs extending equal coverage of accident legislation to farm workers. If the states fail to extend coverage to these workers, the federal government should do so, as it has with longshoremen and in the District of Columbia.

The National Commission on State Workmen's Compensation Laws has recommended that farm workers be covered on the same basis as other workers. But because of "administrative considerations," the commission recommended a two-stage approach: "As of August 1, 1973, coverage should be extended to agricultural employees whose employer's annual payroll exceeds $1,000. By July 1, 1975, coverage should be extended to farm workers on the same basis as all other employees" (National Commission, *Report*, 1971, p. 17).

REFERENCES

"Agricultural Minimum Wage Coverage Impact." *Farm Labor Developments* (May 1968).

Coles, Robert. "Statement to Subcommittee on Migratory Labor." In *The Migratory Farm Labor Problem in the United States.* Washington, D.C.: U.S. Government Printing Office. 1969.

Janson, Donald. "Minimum Wages Elude U.S. Farm Help." New York *Times.* September 12, 1971.

Lovell, Malcolm. "A Commitment to Serve Rural America." Remarks to the National Rural Manpower Conference, Atlanta, January 18, 1971.

National Commission on State Workmen's Compensation Laws. *Report of the National Commission.* Washington, D.C. 1971.

National Safety Council. *Accident Facts.* Washington, D.C. 1967.

"The Farm Worker and Unemployment Insurance." *Rural Manpower Developments* (September-October 1971).

U.S. Department of Labor. *Hired Farm Workers: A Study of the Effects of the $1.15 Minimum Wage under the Fair Labor Standards Act.* Washington, D.C.: U.S. Department of Labor, Wage and Hour and Public Contracts Division. 1969.

7. Summary and Conclusions

THIS BOOK HAS outlined current agricultural and industrial development in rural areas; discussed the nature of some problems confronting rural workers; examined the effectiveness of some rural manpower programs; explored the prospects of unions, community development corporations, and cooperatives as organizations to represent the interests of rural workers and promote rural development; and discussed the inadequacies of protective legislation for agricultural workers. The fact was also emphasized that rural development has important implications for the welfare of urban as well as rural people.

Current trends in agriculture are displacing many workers, with little effort to help them prepare for emerging farm or nonfarm employment. Technological change is the main catalyst, but U.S. agricultural policy has subsidized technological change and contributed to the displacement of small farmers and agricultural workers by land, capital, and other subsidies which favor larger farmers who, contrary to popular impression, do not have across-the-board economies of size over smaller family farms. Because of their low levels of education, training, and nonfarm work experience and the declining demand for semiskilled and unskilled nonfarm labor, many of those workers who are being displaced are remaining in rural areas, while others are migrating to urban areas, particularly during times of full employment in the national economy.

Many of those who migrate to urban areas join the ranks of the urban poor and contribute to urban congestion and social problems, even though they would prefer to stay in rural areas if they could find jobs there. Because manufacturing employment is actually growing

171

faster in rural than in urban areas, many of those who are completely or partially displaced from agriculture find nonfarm jobs. However, industrialization has had limited benefits for many unemployed and underemployed rural residents, because the firms coming in bring workers with them, attract them from other areas, "skim" local labor supplies, or pay wages so low that workers are not able to earn enough to raise them above the poverty level. Although the dimensions of the problem are not known, there also is considerable racial discrimination by rural nonfarm employers in the South.

Among the most disadvantaged rural workers are the migrants, many of whom are blacks and chicanos. Migrants suffer many disabilities associated with their mobility and the conditions under which they live and work. However, the dimensions of the migrant problem are being reduced by mechanization, which has greatly reduced migrant employment. Many measures have been adopted to deal with the problems of migrants, but many of these have had limited effectiveness because they did not get at the root of the problem, namely, the fact that workers were forced by competition from Mexicans and inadequate job opportunities in their home base to travel long distances in order to find employment.

The Labor Department currently is experimenting with a demonstration project to settle migrants out of the migrant stream. However, this is only a partial solution unless the other remedial measures recommended in this book are also adopted. The demand for some migrants undoubtedly will remain, but it is possible to rationalize farm work in such a way as to reduce the extent of migrancy by placing great reliance on local labor supplies. Improved wages and benefits will make these jobs more attractive to nonfarm workers.

It should be emphasized that the problems of rural areas are not solving themselves by "natural" developments. The rural population is *not* declining — it was as large absolutely in 1970 as it was in 1960. The *agricultural* population is declining, but the *rural nonfarm* population is increasing to offset this decline. Moreover, the natural increase in the rural population remains higher than in urban areas. The following rough statistics for 1971 indicate the dimensions of various rural groups:

Category	Million
Rural population	54.00
Rural work force	30.00
Agricultural work force	3.90

Self-employed farmers 1.84
Wage and salary agricultural workers 1.44
Unpaid family farm workers 0.64
Seasonal farm workers 0.82
Migrant farm workers 0.18

Thus it can be seen that despite considerable discussion, the migrant work force actually is only about 13 percent of the hired farm work force and less than a fourth of the seasonal work force.

Various manpower programs have been adopted to help rural workers. Perhaps the most important organizational development was the change in the Farm Labor Service to the Farm Labor and Rural Manpower Service in 1969 and the Rural Manpower Service in 1970. The Rural Manpower Service is trying to change the Farm Labor Service practice of being mainly responsive to agricultural employers by attempting to concern itself with the needs of workers in the total rural setting, rather than just in agriculture. It also is developing programs geared specifically to the needs of rural areas, rather than merely attempting to adapt programs developed mainly in an urban setting.

Rural manpower programs have been limited by the scarcity of manpower experts to write proposals and administer programs, low population densities, limited training facilities, and an apparent urban bias in manpower programs and legislation. The Rural Manpower Service is attempting to gain a greater share of manpower funds for rural areas and seeks to become an advocate for rural manpower within the Labor Department. These measures are movements in the right direction, but the Rural Manpower Service will have to work hard to shake the poor image and eliminate the grower-oriented influences that apparently permeate its field operations. It will be especially important to get more chicano and black staff members to deal with these groups in rural areas. However, its reputation is so bad among some of these groups that it will take more than minority staff members to improve its image. The plan to integrate the Rural Manpower Service into the employment service therefore is probably a good move, but without organizations to represent agricultural and other rural workers, these changes are not likely to be very effective. Unions and cooperatives might accomplish this, but the prospects are not bright for either organization in the present hostile political and economic environment.

Agricultural workers generally have been excluded from such protective legislation as unemployment insurance, workmen's compensation, minimum wages, and collective bargaining. We must conclude that there are no significant substantive reasons for these exclusions and that all of these measures should be extended to agricultural workers who need these benefits more than most nonfarm workers. The main reason for their exclusion is their powerlessness, which is hardly a social justification for discrimination.

Because there are so few spokesmen for the rural poor, it is particularly important to encourage collective bargaining and the establishment of other representative organizations among rural workers.

POLICY IMPLICATIONS

The main policy implication of the analyses of this book is that economic development depends heavily on the quality of human resource development. The kinds of activities likely to promote rural human resource development include:

(1) Improvements in the quantity and quality of rural education, especially vocational-technical education to prepare people for nonfarm as well as farm jobs. Since low-income rural areas have limited ability to finance quality education, local financing will perpetuate rural disadvantages. Financing therefore should be on a national basis because migration makes the quality of work forces a national problem.

(2) Rural manpower programs to provide a better match between workers and jobs. These manpower programs include measures to provide more and better labor market information and job training. Rural areas participated in manpower programs during the 1960s but not as much as urban areas in proportion to their need or population. This lack of access to manpower resources was due in part to the difficulties in extending manpower services to scattered rural populations; insufficient training facilities, especially for on-the-job training; limited job opportunities for those who were trained; and a paucity of leadership to fight for manpower resources and to administer those programs that get funded.

These problems can be overcome by six possible remedies. First, measures to increase and assure more equitable access to manpower resources should be explored. This can be accomplished by formula allocations to substitute for the political weaknesses of those needing rural manpower development resources. The formula should be more indicative of human resource needs than the unemployment rate, which does not measure people who would work if jobs were available, part-time workers, working heads of poverty households, or those working below their skill levels.

Second, procedures to gear manpower programs to the unique problems of rural areas should be developed. These include efforts to compensate for the paucity of rural manpower agencies by attaching manpower services to such existing entities as farmers' organizations, chambers of commerce, multicounty units of government, cooperatives, and workers' organizations.

Third, manpower programs should be closely coordinated with economic development activities. These programs can be used for such diverse functions as training managers for low-income cooperatives, training small farmers in marketable nonfarm skills, building an information base in local labor markets as an inducement to the location of industry in those areas, training and relocating people who are not likely to find suitable employment in a particular labor market, training workers in appropriate occupations as an inducement for certain industry to locate in a particular area, and providing public employment for those who are not likely to benefit from industrialization or relocation.

Evidence in this book suggests that unskilled people recently or incompletely removed from agriculture are unlikely to improve their incomes unless they increase their skills and productivity. Unfortunately, however, too much "training" during the 1960s was ineffective because it was either really income maintenance or preparation for nonexisting jobs. An approach which gives promise of promoting a better match between jobs paying the poverty wage and training is the so-called "start-up" training concept, whereby industrial location and training are closely coordinated.

Fourth, there also is a need for organizations in rural areas to facilitate the development process by adopting strategies and programs representing all of the interests of rural people. Unfortunately, low-income nonfarm workers, small farmers, agricultural workers, and low-income people generally have not been well enough organized to have had much impact on public policy. It therefore would be in the public interest to promote organizations like unions, cooperatives, and community development agencies among these groups and to extend to agricultural workers the benefits of all protective labor legislation available to nonfarm workers. There is a special need for more vigorous enforcement of antidiscrimination laws in rural nonfarm employment in the South.

Fifth, because there are few rural community development agencies, it also would be in the public interest to provide public development coordinators in predominantly rural counties, especially those where subemployment (unemployment, plus discouraged workers not in the work force, plus working heads of poor households) is high. These coordinators could be trained to identify program needs, help local groups formulate development plans, identify available resources, and otherwise act as catalysts for development.

Sixth, in addition to technical assistance there is a need for credit sources to make funds available to small farmers, nonfarm entrepreneurs, cooperatives, and community development corporations.

The objective of rural development should not be to hold people "down on the farm," because agriculture is only one source of rural income and by itself will provide adequate incomes for very few people. Nor should the development of rural nonfarm industry be designed to halt the rural-to-urban migration, because many people, particularly younger people with limited rural attachments, will continue to migrate to urban areas. Rather, a rural development strategy should increase the options available to people and provide better information for making choices.

Public policy in the United States has accelerated the displacement of people through subsidizing technological change, land, and capital, and has done almost nothing to prepare displaced people for change. Rural development policy should make it possible for people who decide to leave rural areas to have the information and access to training and education to facilitate the adjustment. By the same token, public policy should make it possible for those who elect to remain in, or migrate to, rural areas to develop themselves to the point where they can at least earn enough to elevate themselves out of poverty. Such a policy should seek to reduce population pressures on our largest cities by making it possible for more people to remain in rural areas and diverting others to smaller places where jobs exist, help protect the environment by avoiding urban congestion, provide public service jobs to help reduce environmental decay, reduce welfare dependency by making people more self-sufficient, and promote the survival of small farmers who also might be rural nonfarm workers.

We have attempted to demonstrate that rural development is not only possible but also in the national interest. While the displacement of workers from agriculture probably will not be as significant in the future as it has been in the past, rural-urban migration undoubtedly will continue in the future, and many people will also continue to move from urban to rural areas. Public policy can see to it that people have better choices, either to remain in rural areas or to migrate, and that these choices are made on the basis of better information than has been true in the past. Similarly, greater attention to human resource development will make it possible for people to have higher incomes and greater control of their own destinies, whether or not they elect to remain in rural areas.

Index

179